TRANSCULTURAL NURSING

a contemporary imperative

Susan M Dobson RGN RHV PhD(Edin)

Formerly Assistant Professor, College of Nursing,
University of Saskatchewan

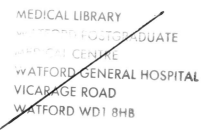
SCUTARI PRESS

London

© Scutari Press 1991

A division of Scutari Projects, the publishing company of the Royal College of Nursing

First published 1991

British Library Cataloguing in Publication Data

Dobson, Susan M.
   Transcultural nursing.
   1. Medicine. Nursing. Implications of cultural differences
   I. Title
   610.73

   ISBN 1-871364-54-X

Typeset, printed and bound by the Alden Press, Osney Mead, Oxford

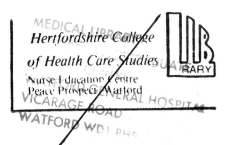
TRANSCULTURAL NURSING

Copyright Permissions

The Publisher and Author wish to acknowledge and thank the following for use of copyright material.

The Italian Catholic Mission, Bedford, England for the photograph (Figure 2) on page 5.

The Ukrainian Museum of Canada, Saskatoon, Saskatchewan for the photograph (Figure 4a) on page 11.

Mr G W Malaher and the Western Development Museum, Saskatoon, Saskatchewan, Canada for the photograph (Figure 4b) on page 11.

The Sisters of Charity (Grey Nuns) of Montreal, Quebec for permission to use the illustration (Figure 5) on page 13.

Lord Lichfield and the VSO (London) for permission to use the photograph (Figure 8) on page 65.

Dr Madeleine Leininger for the photograph (Figure 9) on page 67.

Mrs Liz Gibson and the Montreal Children's Hospital, Quebec for the photograph (Figure 10) on page 74.

Mr David Bocking and the Sheffield Mobile Health Clinic for Travellers for the photograph (Figure 11) on page 83.

Miss Nancy Roper, Dr Winifred Logan and Dr Alison Tierney, and Churchill Livingstone (Edinburgh) for permission to use the Roper, Logan, Tierney model illustrated in Figure 12 on page 84 from *The elements of nursing – A model for nursing based on a model of living* published in 1990.

Mr Peter Wilson and The Star Pheonix, Saskatoon, Saskatchewan, Canada for the photograph (Figure 13) on page 102.

Blackwell Scientific Publications Limited for permission to re-use the author's schema (Figure 14, on page 104) which appeared in an article in the *Journal of Advanced Nursing* in 1989 (Volume 14, pages 97–102), and also in the author's PhD thesis (1987 unpublished).

The Saskatchewan Indian Cultural Centre, Saskatoon for the illustration (Figure 15) on page 106.

Dr Madeleine Leininger and the *Nursing Science Quarterly* published by Williams and Wilkins, Baltimore, USA, for the figure on page 119 (Figure 17).

Dr Modesta S Orque for the figure on page 121 (Figure 18).

Mrs T R Melville-Ness, Saskatoon, Saskatchewan, Canada for the photograph (Figure 19) on page 131.

Nursing Times (London) for permission to re-use the author's figures which first appeared in an article on December 20/27, 1989 (Vol. 85(51): 54–56); Figures 20, 21, 22 on pages 172, 173, 175.

Thanks are also extended to Mr and Mrs Ronald Young of Edinburgh for their kind permission to use the photograph (Figure 7) on page 50.

Dedication

To my mother and father, both my grandmothers and my sister whose love, support, guidance and friendship have meant and continue to mean so much to me.

Contents

Acknowledgements

My acknowledgements go, not only to those who have been supportive of me while I have been writing this book, but also to many friends and family members who have been influential in my life in many wonderful ways and have encouraged me to take on new challenges. I am especially grateful to my mother, Margaret Dobson, who has read through each major draft of the text with immense care and has provided support and criticism from start to finish. Thank you for everything. I also extend my warmest thanks to Nicole Rousseau and Francine Saillant, both of l'Ecole des sciences infirmières, Université Laval, Quebec, Canada; to Nicole for finding time to read drafts of this entire text and for offering helpful criticism and encouragement, and to Francine for reading and commenting upon a later draft of the Use of Terms.

Writing this book has been a voyage of experience, and I would like to extend my deepest thanks to a number of people living in Saskatoon who offered their caring support, especially to: Betty Wood, Florence Lewis, Sophie Bean and Cindy Mathisen. My thanks are also extended to the staff of various organizations who kindly gave me access to their photographic archives, namely, the staff of: the Frances Morrison Library, the Saskatchewan Archives Board, the Ukrainian Museum of Canada, and the Western Development Museums Provincial Service Centre, all of Saskatoon, Canada; also the staff of the Italian Day Nursery, Bedford, and the Voluntary Service Overseas, London, both of England. Acknowledgements of specific material are listed at the beginning of the book. I am also indebted to the staff of the University of Saskatchewan libraries whose helpfulness has been much appreciated.

Finally, special gratitude is due to Rosemary Morris, formerly book publisher for Scutari Press, and to Anne Bassett, director of Scutari Press, for without their unfailing encouragement, guidance and support, this book would never have become a reality.

Preface

With international travel no longer the experience of the few, and with many societies, such as contemporary Britain, indisputably multicultural, nurses in many countries worldwide care for clients from a wide diversity of cultural traditions. Intercultural variations in nurse–client interactions may be manifold. Indeed, the provision of culturally relevant nursing care to multicultural clienteles is a major challenge which the nursing profession faces as it looks to the year 2000 and beyond. Not only may both client and nurse be from a cultural minority group and not from the dominant majority culture of a given country, but each may be from different cultural minorities. It has therefore become imperative for nurses to have a sound understanding of the concept of culture and its relevance to individualized client care. While the provision of care that is relevant to the client's, rather than to the nurse's, cultural perspective is of particular importance as regards nursing that takes place in the client's home, this applies no less to nursing in hospital and clinic settings.

Even when positive efforts are made to link culture to care, unintended, unanticipated and unrecognized difficulties nevertheless occur. To help prevent situations becoming marred by cultural misunderstandings and conflict, nurses need to be skilled in bridging cultural barriers and adept in the discovery of cultural information pertaining to client health. To achieve this, the nurse must be proficient in disengaging from her or his own cultural view and in envisaging life from the client's cultural perspective. In this book, transcultural nursing is presented as an approach to nursing in which nurses actively recognize that each client views health and illness through his, her or its (in the sense of family- or community-as-client) own culture-specific lens. Nursing care is seen to be most effective when congruence with the client's cultural orientation occurs. While simple to advocate, the provision of transculturally sensitive nursing care can nevertheless be difficult to achieve, for instance, if client and nurse fail to accept each other as partners in health care or health promotion, or if nursing's organizational ethos is predominantly unicultural.

The purpose of this book is to help nurses provide transcultural care in intercultural situations. Rather than encouraging the nurse to develop encyclopaedic knowledge of numerous cultural traditions, the aim is that the nurse will become better acquainted with principles and concepts basic to transcultural nursing and feel confident to use them in everyday practice. The format takes the reader from an initial overview of the multicultural context within which nurses in Britain and elsewhere currently practise, to a consideration of culture as a concept intrinsic to both health and nursing. The emergence in recent years of cultural assessment guides attests to the importance of culture as a variable in nursing practice. The reader is invited to consider how nursing care might be provided for clients from a variety of cultural traditions and in various nursing settings. Although cultural variables are the main focus of this text, racial factors are not ignored. The idea of using ethnographic approaches to cultural discovery is put forward and findings from a study of Punjabi families living in Britain in which ethnographic approaches were used are presented and discussed in relation to health visiting practice.

The central focus of this book is the need for nurses practising in multicultural societies worldwide to be proficient in nursing transculturally. In increasing their awareness of clients as cultural beings, nurses can also heighten their awareness of themselves and their nursing colleagues as cultural beings. While essential to nursing in multicultural situations, transcultural empathy and care are also important to the promotion of intercultural and international understanding among nurses, not only in Britain but worldwide. Whether or not they work with major international organizations, such as the International Council of Nurses, the World Council of Churches, Oxfam or the Commonwealth Nurses Federation (among those well known are Sheila Quinn and Margaret Brayton), *all* nurses can be active in promoting cultural understanding among members of the nursing profession as well as in nurse–client relationships if they take time to consider life as viewed from another cultural standpoint. Indeed, looking beyond our own cultural way of life can assume many dimensions, as transcultural nursing is concerned specifically with the provision of culturally appropriate and sensitive nursing care in all areas of nursing practice.

Use of Terms

Because of the centrality of terms such as culture, multicultural, intercultural and ethnic group to the concept and practice of transcultural nursing, a review of terms used in this text is appropriate at this early juncture. Many terms are defined as they are introduced, though the concept of culture is not addressed in depth until Chapter 2. As ideas and viewpoints of various writers are discussed – notably those of nurses, medical practitioners, anthropologists and sociologists – terms may vary as to how they are used by different writers.

Culture is one term that has been variously defined over the years. In this text, the term is used as it relates to ethnic groups. While this concept is not the exclusive property of any one academic discipline, it is central to anthropology.

Despite anthropologists, and other scholars, having produced a plethora of definitions for the concept of culture, commonalities are apparent. Socially inherited and dynamic in nature, cultures are shared entities which have a power of their own and are beyond the control of the individual person. While some scholars place emphasis on the behavioural aspect of culture, others view culture not as 'behavior itself but the shared understandings that guide behavior and are expressed in behavior' (Peacock, 1986: 3). Indeed, culture may be defined as: 'the taken-for-granted but powerfully influential understandings and codes that are learned and shared by members of a group' (ibid: 7). All cultures have both explicit and implicit rules, the latter being much more difficult than the former for an outsider to learn. They also have a specific range of behaviour which members of the group consider to be proper and acceptable

(Haviland, 1987: 27). When cultural rules are transgressed in intercultural nurse–client encounters, situations and relationships can develop which both parties – each used to abiding by different cultural norms and upholding different cultural traditions – find awkward, unsettling and sometimes totally unacceptable (see Bauwens and Anderson, 1988: 90). The concept of culture is defined and discussed further in Chapter 2.

Throughout this text, numerous examples will be found of the adjectival and adverbial forms of the term culture. When the adjectival form **cultural** is used, this is sometimes in reference to the term culture in a general sense, at other times in tacit reference to a particular culture under discussion. We speak of **cultural traditions**, elements of a culture that are singled out by the group as being especially worthy of acceptance and are perpetuated by being handed down from one generation to the next (e.g. Sampson, 1964: 723). We may speak of **cultural knowledge**, knowledge that appertains to one particular, several or many culture/s, and also of **cultural discovery**, a term used in reference to the discovery of cultural information that provides nurses, for example, with insight into, and an understanding of, a given culture or various cultures. Another term, **cultural imposition**, is used in reference to the imposition that members of a cultural group, whether a majority group or a powerful minority group, place on members of a less powerful group, expecting them to change and conform to their ways and expectations. As defined by Leininger (1978: 490), cultural imposition is:

> the tendency of an individual or cultural group to impose their beliefs, values, and patterns of behavior upon another culture for varied reasons, e.g., religious, economical, political, and social.

The adverbial form **culturally** is also used frequently in this text, often in relation to nursing or health care. **Culturally appropriate nursing care**, for example, is advocated throughout and used in reference to nursing care that is appropriate for the client within the context of the client's culture. As nurses are usually expected to practise in accordance with a set of stated ethical parameters drawn up by a professional nursing body in whichever country they work, culturally appropriate nursing care should also be provided to clients, of whatever culture, with due regard to the nurse's code of professional conduct and, indeed, to the International Council of Nurses' (1973) *Code for Nurses*.

Two other terms, **sub-culture** and **culture shock**, involve the use of the term culture. Though minimally used in this text, **sub-culture** has been defined by Leininger (1978: 493) as:

> a group that deviates in certain areas or features with respect to values, beliefs, and behavior from that of a dominant or parent culture with which they are perceived or known to be closely identified in daily life.

Culture shock relates to an 'abrupt transition from a familiar to an alien environment' and involves 'many major and minor differences in life styles and events' (Brink and Saunders, 1976: 127; see also Rack, 1982: 56–8). It occurs when the cultural cues to which we are accustomed and which help us to function in our usual cultural milieu are no longer present but replaced by new ones, for instance when we move to live among members of an ethnic group dissimilar to our own.

Before moving on to discuss other terms relating to the concept of culture, the reader is reminded that for most terms various definitions may be found. Indeed, the reader is encouraged to turn to standard social science encyclopaedias and dictionaries (e.g. Gould and Kolb, 1964; Kuper and Kuper, 1985) to gain greater insight into the different terms, their evolution and their usage in different countries. Many other texts (e.g. Leininger's (1978) *Transcultural Nursing – Concepts, theories, and practices*) also provide useful definitions of terms relevant to transcultural nursing.

Several prefixes are used regularly throughout this text in conjunction with the word 'cultural', notably **inter-**, **intra-**, **multi-** and **trans-**(cultural). 'Intercultural' and 'intracultural' are reasonably self-explanatory. With regard to nursing, the term **intercultural** is used to describe situations, relationships and practice in which the client and the nurse are of different cultural traditions; at times both may be from a different ethnic minority group. **Intracultural** is used when the client and the nurse are of the same cultural tradition. As used by the author, the term **unicultural** relates to an activity, institution, situation or perspective in which the primacy of the dominant culture of a given country is upheld, with only peripheral recognition given to the presence of other cultural groups within that society. The term **monocultural** is used occasionally, and carries the same meaning as unicultural.

Multicultural, as used by the author in reference to her own ideas but not necessarily those of other writers, is used to imply the presence of, or in reference to, more than one culture, for instance with regard to societies and nursing situations. The use of the term **transcultural** also depends on whether it is being used in relation to the author's ideas regarding nursing practice or in reference to the ideas of other writers. When used in relation to the author's ideas, the term transcultural should be understood not only as implying the presence of, or in reference to, more than one culture, but also as denoting the coexistence of an affirmative desire to bridge and transcend cultural differences within the nurse–client relationship. When used in reference to the ideas of other writers, the term should be understood as defined by the writer in question. To avoid unnecessary multiplicity of similar terms, the term **cross-cultural** is used only in relation to ideas and texts of other authors.

The term **biculturalism** is used occasionally, in relation to Canada and New Zealand. For a country/society to uphold biculturalism, members of that country/society aim to preserve and enhance two cultures, lifestyles and sets of values (see Bauwens and Anderson, 1988: 92). In discussing New Zealand, biculturalism is used in reference to the Maori and the Pakeha (the non-Maori), and as regards Canada, to the anglophone and the francophone populations.

It is also important that nurses caring for multicultural clienteles have an understanding of terms relating to ethnic status and race. The adjective **ethnic**, used many times throughout this text, is derived from the Greek word *ethnos* meaning 'people' or 'nation' (Gordon, 1964: 24). An important term is **ethnic group**, a descent group with a common culture. To form 'a real ethnic group' and not 'a mere ethnic collection of people', Smooha (1985: 267) indicates that the members must, to some degree, 'perceive themselves as a distinct ethnic group ("we" and "they" feelings), sense a common fate, interact more among themselves than with outsiders, and think and behave similarly.' While there is 'no acceptable single word in English for the phrase "ethnic group"', that is, 'no word equivalent to "class", "caste", or "family" to describe a group self-consciously united around particular cultural traditions', De Vos (1975: 9) observes that French anthropologists have suggested 'the word *ethne* for technical usage'.

Ethnicity is another term linked to the notion of ethnic status, but is minimally used in this text. A somewhat elusive concept, which Gordon (1964: 24) saw as a convenient way to describe a 'sense of peoplehood' and Glazer and Moynihan (1975: 1) considered to be a term 'still on the move', ethnicity is part of an individual's social identity and may be based on a variety of factors, including past origins, language or religion (Sorofman, 1986: 121). The extent to which ethnic groups manifest their ethnicity varies from group to group (Cohen, 1974: xiv), ethnicity crystallizing 'only in situations where people of different backgrounds come into contact or share the same institutions or political system' (Smooha, 1985: 267).

Ethnocentrism is yet another term with which nurses should be familiar. Sumner (1907: 13), who originally developed the concept of ethnocentrism, defines it as a 'view of things in which one's own group is the center of everything, and all others are scaled and rated with reference to it'. Ethnocentrism finds emotional expression among members of an ethnic group in 'a sympathetic awareness and approval' of the members of the group and their ways and a feeling of 'fear, suspicion and contempt' towards outsiders and their ways (Murdock, 1931: 613). To hold an ethnocentric viewpoint is to consider that one's own culture 'represents the best, or at least the most appropriate, way for human beings to live' (Spradley and McCurdy, 1977: 3). All of us are to some degree ethnocentric, and eliminating or reducing cultural bias is a challenge that nurses face when they render care to clients from cultures other than their own (Brown, 1980: 69).

While this book specifically addresses transcultural nursing, intercultural nursing may involve racial as well as cultural disparities (and indeed, other disparities such as class) between nurse and client. Though taxonomies exist to classify mankind into various **races**, there is no universally accepted classification system (Rack, 1982: 15–18, 21–23). Indeed, the **race** to which a person is considered to belong depends greatly on the perception, by that person and by others, of physical differences such as skin pigmentation and bone structure. The significance given to particular physical features may vary from country to country. The term 'black', for instance, is frequently used in the United Kingdom to encompass all non-whites, whether of West Indian, African or Asian heritage (e.g. Runnymede Trust, 1980), yet this would not necessarily be the situation in Brazil, Cuba or Jamaica, where, according to Banton (1987: 355) 'a coffee-coloured person' would not be assigned to a black racial group. In the United States, however, 'white, yellow, red, brown and black' are recognized as labels for 'racial stocks' where skin colour is the criterion (Ruffin, 1979: 3).

Although the scientific validity of the concept of race is open to question, race nevertheless is a powerful social labelling device. The Black Report (DHSS, 1980: 26) states that 'one of the most important dimensions of inequality in contemporary Britain is race'. Indeed, Rack (1982: 17), writing about Britain, suggests that 'colour' is 'the greatest single factor which governs society's attitude to members of minority groups', an 'inescapable' factor which 'influences their own self-image'.

Racism is another important term and may be defined as 'a mixed form of prejudice (attitude) and discrimination (behavior) directed at ethnic groups other than one's own' (Herberg, 1989: 52; see also Mares, Henley and Baxter, 1985: 5). Whether occurring at an institutional or personal level, and whether unintentional or deliberate, racism is a reality that shapes the lives and health care experiences of many members of ethnic minority groups that are also racial minorities (e.g. Brent Community Health Council, 1981; Iskander, 1987; Baxter, 1989).

While the question of racism, as it relates to the service health care professionals offer, is addressed in 'racial' terminology within the British nursing/health literature (e.g. Ellis, 1978; Knight, 1978; Pearson, 1986), different terminology may be used in other countries, for example, in Canada and the United States (e.g. under the rubric of 'ethnicity' (Rootman, 1988: 5–6), or as 'ethnic people of color' (Branch and Paxton, 1976)). Indeed, the reader should bear in mind that terms relevant to the concept and practice of transcultural nursing may be used differently and assume differing connotations in different countries. Other examples include the terms 'black' and 'ethnic minority' sometimes being used interchangeably in British literature (e.g. Satow and Homans, 1981), and in the United States the term 'ethnic group' being equated with 'ethnic minority group', while members of US ethnic groups are sometimes referred to as 'ethnics' (e.g. Novak, 1972).

Though the use of the term 'native' for the aboriginal or indigenous population of Canada and the United States is accepted practice in North America, it is not an expression commonly used in Britain. In Canada, the native Indian is a member of one of the aboriginal groups or tribes (also known as the First Nations) of North America such as the Cree, the Mohawk and the Haida, whereas the person from India is known as an 'East Indian' (and as an 'Asian Indian' in the United States [Allen and Turner, 1988: 198–200]). The native Indian of Canada may also be described as a status Indian, that is a person of native ancestry who is registered, or entitled to be registered, as an Indian under the Indian Act which both defines 'the criteria for registration as a status Indian' and describes 'the rights and obligations involved' (Statistics Canada, 1984: [3]; also Canada, 1985; Woodward, 1989: 7). A non-status Indian, however, is a person 'with some degree of Indian blood and culture' but who falls 'outside the statutory definition of an Indian in the Indian Act' (Woodward, 1989: 58). Reference is also made to the Inuit and the Métis of Canada. Sharing a distinct culture, the Inuit are an aboriginal group of people who, for the most part, live north of the tree line, whereas the Métis are descendants of people of mixed aboriginal and European ancestry who formed a distinct cultural group in the nineteenth century (Statistics Canada, 1984: [3]).

As the need for cultural appropriateness and sensitivity becomes increasingly accepted as intrinsic to the provision of nursing care in multicultural societies, so nurses will become more accustomed to using a variety of terms and concepts which have their roots in anthropology, comparative religion and sociology. The concept of cultural pollution or impurity, for example, may be new to many nurses, yet is central to various secular and religious beliefs and rituals of many cultures worldwide. In some cultures, for example, parts of the body are viewed in terms of purity and impurity, cleanness and uncleanness. For some, the head is considered the purest part of the body, and the right hand cleaner in cultural terms than the left hand. Both Douglas (e.g. 1966) and Hershman (e.g. 1974, in regard to Punjabi culture) have written at length on this topic. A number of cultural groups believe in the 'evil eye', a belief that may also be new to some nurses. Rather than being a single belief, the idea of the evil eye is a cluster of beliefs 'whose only common factor is a conviction that a person's inner qualities and intentions can emanate from his eyes' (Maloney, 1976: 134). Once again the reader is encouraged to turn to social science dictionaries and encyclopaedias as well as to pertinent references provided in the text and elsewhere to become better acquainted with the various definitions and uses of concepts and terms rooted in anthropology and sociology which have relevance to transcultural nursing.

REFERENCES

Allen JP and Turner EJ (1988) *We the people. An Atlas of America's Ethnic Diversity*. New York: Macmillan.

Banton M (1987) What we now know about race. *New Community* **13**(3): 349–58

Bauwens E and Anderson S (1988) Social and cultural influences on health care. In M Stanhope and J Lancaster (eds), *Community*

Health Nursing. Process and practice for promoting health, 2nd edn. St Louis: CV Mosby.

Baxter C (1989) Race and child abuse. *Health Visitor* **62**(9): 271–2.

Branch MF and Paxton PP (eds) (1976) *Providing Safe Nursing Care for Ethnic People of Color*. New York: Appleton-Century-Crofts.

Brent Community Health Council (1981) *Black People and the Health Service*. London: Brent Community Health Council.

Brink PJ and Saunders JM (1976) Cultural shock. Theoretical and applied. In PJ Brink (ed.), *Transcultural Nursing. A book of readings*. Englewood Cliffs, NJ: Prentice Hall.

Brown H (1980) Ethnocentrism in nursing. Breakthrough. *Imprint* **27**(1): 26, 69.

Canada (1985) Revised Statutes of Canada. *Indian Act*, R.S., c. 1–6, s. 1.

Cohen A (1974) Introduction. In A Cohen (ed.), *Urban Ethnicity*. London: Tavistock.

De Vos G (1975) Ethnic pluralism. Conflict and accommodation. In G De Vos and L Romanucci-Ross (eds), *Ethnic Identity. Cultural continuities and change*. Palo Alto, CA: Mayfield.

DHSS (Department of Health and Social Security) (1980) *Inequalities in Health*. Report of a research working group. Chairman: Sir Douglas Black. London: DHSS.

Douglas M (1966) *Purity and Danger. An analysis of the concepts of pollution and taboo*. London: Routledge & Kegan Paul.

Ellis S (1978) That unspoken prejudice. *Nursing Times* **74**(48): 1964–5.

Glazer N and Moynihan DP (1975) Introduction. In N Glazer and DP Moynihan (eds), *Ethnicity. Theory and experience*. Cambridge, MA: Harvard University Press.

Gordon MM (1964) *Assimilation in American Life*. New York: Oxford University Press.

Gould J and Kolb WL (eds) (1964) *A Dictionary of the Social Sciences*. London: Tavistock.

Haviland WA (1987) *Cultural Anthropology*, 5th edn. New York: Holt, Rinehart & Winston.

Herberg P (1989) Theoretical foundations of transcultural nursing. In JS Boyle and MM Andrews (eds), *Transcultural Concepts in Nursing Care*. Glenview, IL: Scott, Foresman.

Hershman P (1974) Hair, sex and dirt. *Man (NS)* **9**(2): 274–98.

International Council of Nurses (1973) *Code for Nurses. Ethical concepts applied to nursing*. Geneva: International Council of Nurses.

Iskander R (1987) Developing a black consciousness. *Nursing Times* **83** (42): 66, 69.

Knight L (1978) Protect their minds too. *Mind Out*, No. 31: 12–14.

Kuper A and Kuper J (eds) (1985) *The Social Science Encyclopedia*. London: Routledge & Kegan Paul.

Leininger M (ed.) (1978) *Transcultural Nursing. Concepts, theories, and practices*. New York: John Wiley.

Maloney C (1976) Don't say 'Pretty baby' lest you zap it with your eye. The evil eye in South Asia. In (C Maloney (ed.), *The Evil Eye*. New York: Columbia University Press.

Mares P, Henley A and Baxter C (1985) *Health Care in Multiracial Britain*. Cambridge: Health Education Council/National Extension College.

Murdock GP (1931) Ethnocentrism. In ER Seligman (ed.), *Encyclopaedia of the Social Sciences*, **5**. London: Macmillan.

Novak M (1972) *The Rise of the Unmeltable Ethnics*. New York: Macmillan.

Peacock JL (1986) *The Anthropological Lens. Harsh light, soft focus*. Cambridge: Cambridge University Press.

Pearson M (1986) Ten years on. *Senior Nurse* 4(4): 18–19.

Rack P (1982) *Race, Culture, and Mental Disorder*. London: Tavistock.

Rootman I (1988) Inequities in health: sources and solutions. *Health Promotion*. Winter: 2–8.

Ruffin JE (1979) Changing perspectives on ethnicity and health. In *A Strategy for Change*. Papers presented at the conference held on 9–10 June at Albuquerque, NM, by the American Nurses' Association Commission on Human Rights.

Runnymede Trust and the Radical Statistics Race Group (1980) *Britain's Black Population*. London: Heinemann.

Sampson RV (1964) Tradition. In J Gould and W L Kolb (eds), *A Dictionary of the Social Sciences*. London: Tavistock.

Satow A and Homans H (1981) Integration or isolation? *Journal of Community Nursing*, October, **5**(4): 4–5, 26.

Smooha S (1985) Ethnic groups. In A Kuper and J Kuper (eds), *The Social Science Encyclopedia*. London: Routledge & Kegan Paul.

Sorofman B (1986) Research in cultural diversity. Defining diversity. *Western Journal of Nursing Research* 8(1): 121–3.

Spradley JP and McCurdy DW (eds) (1977) *Conformity and Conflict. Readings in cultural anthropology*, 3rd edn. Boston, MA: Little, Brown.

Statistics Canada (1984) *Canada's Native People*. 1981 Census of Canada. No. CS99-937. Ottawa: Minister of Supply and Services Canada.

Sumner WG (1907) *Folkways*. Boston, MA: Ginn & Co.

Woodward J (1989) *Native Law*. Toronto: Carswell.

CHAPTER 1

The Multicultural Society and Nursing

INTRODUCTION

For many centuries, explorers, traders, adventurers and missionaries have journeyed to distant lands, many setting out by ship, some on foot, others by camel or horse. Plying the high seas, tea clippers, Viking longships, Arabian dhows and Polynesian outriggers have sailed from Europe, the Middle East and Polynesia to the Orient and the Occident. Innumerable caravans have followed the Silk Road from China to the lands of the Mediterranean. Today, planes traverse the skies, and networks of highways and railways carry goods and people across continents. Mankind has scarcely left a portion of the world unvisited and unexplored, and thus has discovered the vast kaleidoscope of human cultures that spans the globe.

Various motives have led people to travel far afield. While evangelism has spurred both Muslim and Christian to introduce their religion to others worldwide, imperialism has motivated countries such as Belgium, France, the Netherlands, Spain and the United Kingdom to colonize parts of South East Asia, Africa, South America and the West Indies. Requiring raw commodities for their industries and workers for their factories, industrial magnates of the nineteenth century looked to distant lands. Indeed, it was to her colonies that Britain turned for workers to help regenerate her industries and social support services following the Second World War. As a consequence, British society became, and remains, indisputably multicultural. Numerous other countries worldwide are also multicultural societies. The United States of America and Canada, for instance, have developed into multicultural societies and might be described as ethnic/cultural mosaics, each society comprising numerous 'ethnic tiles' (Driedger, 1978: 14) and reflecting a diversity of cultural heritages. In both countries, the aboriginal peoples have become cultural and racial minorities in a land where they once were numerically dominant. In more recent years, countries such as India, the United Kingdom, Australia and Canada have accepted political refugees, so adding to the cultural diversity of their own country.

With opportunities for employment still luring many to distant lands, and vacationing abroad having become commonplace for many in affluent societies, international travel is no longer the experience of the few. Nurses have long travelled, and still travel, abroad to care for people from cultures alien to their own. But today, nurses do not need to travel to nurse people culturally different from themselves, for in many countries nursing 'at home' now assumes international dimensions. Indeed, in the United Kingdom, United States and Australia, nurses care for clients from a wide diversity of cultural backgrounds. As a consequence, proficiency in providing culturally-sensitive nursing care has become essential if codes of professional conduct (e.g. ICN, 1973; UKCC, 1984) are to be upheld.

While the British nursing profession has only recently begun to take a closer look at the importance of providing culturally sensitive care for all, US nurses began to address this concern some years ago (e.g. Leininger, 1967). Important though it is, surmounting linguistic and cultural differences is invariably fraught with difficulties for both client and practitioner. Not only may interpreters with appropriate expertise be unavailable, but practitioners may have little insight into how concepts of health and illness can differ from one culture to another. Difficulties may also arise if ethnic minority clients view the health services as racially and culturally prejudiced (e.g. Cottle, 1977). Nevertheless, providing culturally appropriate nursing care is an exciting challenge, and one that the nurse of today, whether practitioner, educator, researcher or administrator, cannot and should not ignore. As members of an ever-changing society (e.g. Auld, 1979), nurses have to be responsive to society's changing needs, including those relating to variations in ethnic mix.

In this chapter, aspects relating to the multicultural composition of various countries worldwide, particularly the United Kingdom, Canada and the United States, will be considered. The reader is invited to use the references to this chapter for further information about the countries discussed here, and other countries worldwide.

UNITED KINGDOM

The multi-ethnic composition of cities such as London, Birmingham and Bradford and towns such as Bedford is well known (Brown, 1970; Open University, 1982), yet most towns throughout the United Kingdom have populations that, to some extent, are ethnically diverse. The Chinese takeaway and the Indo-Pakistani corner shop, for instance, are common features of contemporary British life. But those who manage or are employed in these enterprises usually form only a small part of the multi-ethnic composition of the localities in which they live. Today, ethnic minority citizens, many of whom are the children and grandchildren of earlier immigrants, are an integral part of British society. Yet racial and cultural distinctiveness continues to debar many from being socially accepted by the indigenous, white Briton.

Although transcultural nursing is a recent focus in British nursing, there is extensive literature for the nurse interested in the development and traditions of Britain's many ethnic minority groups. By way of example, articles and texts are to be found which focus on the Sikhs of Cardiff (Ghuman, 1980) and Leeds (Ballard, 1972), the Pakistanis of Rochdale (Anwar, 1979) and Dundee (Jones and Davenport, 1972), and the Montserratians (Philpott, 1977) and Greek

Fig. 1   One of the largest Chinese communities in Britain is to be found
in central London, in and around Gerrard Street

Cypriots (Constantinides, 1977) of London. More widely
dispersed ethnic populations such as the gypsies (Okely,
1983) and the Chinese (Jackson and Garvey, 1974; Watson,
1977) have also received attention. Most of these texts have
been written by social scientists, i.e. sociologists, anthropologists, geographers and the like. Much less has been
written with the intent of discovering cultural factors that
have specific relevance to nursing care.

Immigration to Britain is not a twentieth-century phenomenon. French Huguenots found sanctuary in England at
various times, especially during the late seventeenth century, and tens of thousands of Irish, forced by famine to seek
a livelihood elsewhere, emigrated to Britain in the 1840s.
During the last quarter of the nineteenth century and until
the early 1900s, European Jews, seeking refuge from persecution especially in Tsarist Russia, settled in various parts
of the country, particularly in Spitalfields in London's East
End (e.g. Eyles, 1982).

Britain has actively encouraged immigration in times of
economic need, notably in the 1950s and 1960s when workers
were needed to help regenerate British industries after the
Second World War and to staff expanding service sectors.

Italians, for example, were employed in the brick factories of Bedford, West Indians in service sectors as bus conductors, enrolled nurses and hospital ancillaries (Brent Community Health Council, 1981; Pearson, 1987), and Gujeratis from India and Mirpuris from Pakistan in the mills of Bolton and Bradford (Saifullah Khan, 1977; Hahlo, 1980).

Fig. 2 Italian Day Nursery, Bedford, c. 1960

Many of the jobs that ethnic minority immigrants undertook in the 1950s and 1960s were poorly paid and involved long and unsocial hours – work that many of the indigenous British preferred not to do. As well as enduring harsh working conditions, many faced the added stress of racial and cultural discrimination. Such forms of discrimination are not new in British society. During the reign of Elizabeth I, 'negroes and blackamoors', by proclamation, were to be speedily expelled from England (File and Power, 1981: 6). In the early twentieth century, Jews were among those considered 'aliens', and whose entry into Britain became restricted with the passing of the Aliens Act in 1905 (see Eyles,

1982: 283). Less than favourable portraits of ethnic minority people are to be found in various writings over the past century. Salter writes of the 'Asiatic in England': 'Artifice and deception are too often the common modes of procedure with the cringing mendicant from the sunny land' (Salter, 1873: 221).

Racist attitudes persist today, with the health service seemingly no exception (Agbolegbe, 1984; Torkington, 1987). The fact that a Creole nurse from Jamaica, Mary Seacole, cared, as did Florence Nightingale, for British soldiers in the Crimea is largely forgotten (Gordon, 1975). Yet exemplary nursing care has always been provided by nurses from countries the world over.

Fig. 3   A Polish Club in Bedford, 1990

Patterns of migration and settlement of differing ethnic minority groups vary considerably: many Poles settled in Britain as exiles after the Second World War, as did East African Asians after they were forced out of Kenya and Uganda in the 1960s and 1970s, respectively. The Vietnamese 'boat people' arrived in the late 1970s (Mares, 1982). West Indians, a term which encompasses the people from islands in the Caribbean such as Barbados, Jamaica and St Kitts, were among those encouraged to take up employment in Britain during the 1950s and 1960s. Indian, Pakistani and Bangladeshi communities have an extended history which can be usefully divided into four main chronological phases, different groups reaching differing stages at different times (Ballard and Ballard, 1977):

1. Pioneer days – mostly seamen and peddlars who were to be the forerunners of the post-war migrations.
2. 1950s – mass migration, initially all-male households followed by reunion of families.
3. 1960s – consolidation of settlements.
4. 1970s – emergence of the second generation.

The Bengali Sylheti are one of the last groups to have arrived from the Indian Subcontinent, but many wives and children are still waiting to join their husbands and fathers in Britain.

In many instances, the term 'immigrant' is used pejoratively to refer, implicitly if not explicitly, to black rather than white persons. Used correctly, it is an important factor in health care, for immigration brings its attendant stresses and strains, whether the immigrant is white or black, and if he or she is from a cultural background that differs markedly from that of the host society (e.g. Rack, 1978).

Many first-generation immigrants have had to cope with the trauma of being far from their families, experiencing marked climatic and environmental changes, and, for some, with ineradicable memories of persecution and tragic losses – political, human and economic (see Fink, 1979; Mares, 1982). As immigrants often need some support, nurses can help to ensure that these needs are met, whether by ethnic-specific self-help groups, by community workers who specialize in immigrant or refugee care, or by other appropriate health care workers.

While not facing the same traumas and dislocations that their parents or grandparents faced, members of second and subsequent generations may nevertheless have serious identity concerns. Born and raised in the United Kingdom, they frequently find they are not readily accepted by members of the dominant culture, yet have little, if any, knowledge of the countries of their ethnic heritage. For many, racial factors pertaining to the 'white British–black British' dichotomy loom large and are very real. The Polish exile who married a white English woman after the Second World War is likely to have had more success in integrating socially into the majority, and predominantly white, culture than is a second-generation West Indian who speaks Creole.

The UKCC (1984) code of professional conduct enjoins the nurse, midwife and health visitor to recognize the importance of clients' and patients' cultural traditions in everyday practice. Although one speaks of a dominant majority culture of the United Kingdom, British society comprises four main cultural groups that follow national lines: the English, the Scots, the Irish and the Welsh. But what are their cultural norms and how might these four cultures be described to a stranger? Are they anything more than stereotypes, which imply a sense of nationhood rather than a cultural identity? A sense of national identity is certainly real, both at a political level and in relation to nursing. Scottish health visitors, for example, have their own association and their own journal, *Focus*, which brings to its readers' attention aspects of health visiting in Scotland. But how does Scottish culture differ from that of the English or the Irish? Are the eating habits of schoolchildren in Edinburgh (Rousseau, 1983) so different from those of schoolchildren in Ipswich, Belfast or Bristol? Do wide variations exist, for instance, within Wales regarding Welsh culture? In what ways did the children from Welsh-speaking homes in Cardiff on whom the Denver developmental screening test was standardized by Bryant, Davies and Newcombe (1979) differ from those of children in Welsh-speaking homes in other areas of the principality, or indeed from non-Welsh-speaking children in Cardiff? Are there any truly substantial differences between the English, the Scots, the Irish and the Welsh cultures? If so, what are they, and how relevant are they to nursing care?

British society became indisputably multicultural, and indeed multiracial, during the 1950s and 1960s. Other countries have also evolved into multicultural societies but in different ways, each country having its unique history. Canada and the United States are two countries which from their earliest beginnings were settled by people of various cultural heritages. In the following two sections, features pertaining to the multicultural nature of both these countries will be discussed.

CANADA

Comprising people from many cultural heritages from all parts of the world, Canada may aptly be described as an ethnic/cultural mosaic. A country with two official languages, French and English, its indigenous peoples, the Inuit and the Indian, are now ethnic/cultural minorities. In recent years, within the framework of bilingualism, Canada has moved towards the notion of multiculturalism (England, 1986), a notion now enshrined in Canadian constitutional law. The Canadian Multiculturalism Act (Bill C-93 – Canada, House of Commons), passed in July 1988, aims to preserve and enhance the multicultural nature of Canada. Recent emphasis has also been placed on reducing inequities in health, including those linked to ethnicity. This is viewed as a national concern, which must be addressed if 'achieving health for all' is to be realized (Health and Welfare Canada, 1986; Rootman, 1988). As Canada moves towards the next millennium, there is an increasing awareness that if health and nursing care are to be effective in the long term for the recipient, then they must be culturally meaningful, whether delivered in the home, the clinic or the hospital setting. Even so, 'Canadian data on health conditions and prospects' at present seldom distinguish between the 'various ethnic, racial and cultural groups' concerned (Rootman, 1988: 5), a notable exception being the status Indian. Should this continue, many inequities linked to ethnicity are likely to remain submerged, minimally explored and unchecked.

Montreal and Toronto are well known for their ethnically diverse populations, as are many cities and towns throughout Canada. Though Canadians come from many ethnic groups (e.g. Richmond, 1969: 10), the arrival, dispersal, acceptance (e.g. Hutterites, a predominantly German-speaking branch of the Mennonite religion: see Dyck, 1981: 240–1) and rejection (e.g. Chinese labourers after the building of the railroad through the Rocky Mountains: CBC, 1981) have led to variations in the country's ethnic mix at different times and in different localities. The use of hyphenated ethnic forms, such as Dutch-Canadians, French-Canadians and, more recently, Indo-Canadians (used in reference to people from India: see Anderson, 1985) – persists, though marriage between members of different ethnic groups has led to a blurring of ethnic divisions and distinctiveness in subsequent generations.

In various parts of the country, certain ethnic groups have tended, and still tend, to predominate. Many of Canada's Ukrainian and Icelandic communities, for example, are to be found on the Prairies, West Indian communities in Toronto, Montreal and Halifax, and French-Canadians in the province of Quebec (although there are numerous French-Canadians residing throughout Canada). Many of the predominantly Chinese quarters ('Chinatowns') of cities such as Vancouver were formed as long ago as the nineteenth century, when Chinese immigrants found the presence of ethnic discrimination and prejudice increased their need to find respite and support within their own community (CBC, 1981).

Ways of bringing culturally appropriate health information and nursing care to Canada's various ethnic groups, including those whose lack of proficiency in English or French impedes ease of access to health care services and the vocalization of consumer preferences, is a concern that the Canadian nursing and health care literature has addressed and continues to address (e.g. Drakulic and Tanaka, 1981; Kendall, 1983; Yoshida and Davies, 1985; Kulig, 1988a and b; Waxler-Morrison, Anderson and Richardson, 1990). Kulig (1988a), for instance, looked at cultural knowledge held by Cambodian refugee women regarding conception and foetal development, with a view to how this might relate to birth control measures and prenatal care. Kendall (1983), also concerned with prenatal education, describes the use of video programmes to channel prenatal education in three Asian languages (Hindi, Punjabi and Cantonese) through local cable television in Vancouver, and presents findings of a post-broadcast survey.

(a) Traditional Ukrainian Bread-making 1990

(b) A Doukhobor Family 1909

Fig. 4 Perpetuating the Ukrainian Heritage

Canadian nursing has its roots in the care given and the establishments set up by French Roman Catholic orders as far back as the seventeenth century, the Grey Nuns being one order well known for its dedication to providing care for the sick and destitute in both community and hospital settings (Gibbon, 1947: 42–9). The importance of cultural factors in patient and client care is well recognized within Canadian nursing. Yet many basic nursing texts still draw predominantly on the ideas and findings of researchers and theorists from the United States (such as Leininger, e.g. 1978; Orque, 1983), and do not reflect the Canadian multicultural scene and hence are of less value in socializing the student nurse into the Canadian milieu than they might otherwise be. Cardenas and Lucarz (1985) offer one of the few contributions in standard North American (including Canadian) nursing texts which provides a description of nursing in multicultural and native settings in Canada – in this instance, in relation to Cree Indians. For the Cree, who traditionally consider health to embrace mind, body and spirit, health is viewed as a state of harmony.

In recent years, the journal *The Canadian Nurse* has become bilingual, some articles being written in English, others in French and all with an abstract in the other language. Most other Canadian nursing journals are produced in English, though *Nursing Québec*, the journal of the Quebec provincial association, the *Ordre des infirmières et infirmiers du Québec* (OIIQ), is written almost entirely in French. The majority of articles on cultural concerns to be found in the Canadian nursing literature over the past several years relates to the needs of visible (less euphemistically, racial) minorities, such as the Cambodians, East Indians (i.e. from India, and also called Indo-Canadians), the Inuit and the Canadian Indians. Although the Canadian nursing literature thus regularly addresses the needs of racial minorities, terms such as 'race' and 'racism' are seldom used. In fact, the possibility of racism being an issue relevant to nursing practice, and to nursing in general, seems to have been generally overlooked or ignored.

Native Indian and Inuit nurses, who numbered approximately 200 in the late 1970s (IINC [n.d., *c.* 1985]: 4), have their

Fig. 5 Grey Nuns: Sisters of Charity of Montreal, Quebec, 1755

own association, the Indian and Inuit Nurses of Canada (IINC). Formed in 1974, and known until 1983 as the Registered Nurses of Canadian Indian Ancestry, this organization seeks to promote and strive for health for the Inuit and Indian people, and to recruit more people of Inuit and native Indian ancestry into the medical field and health professions (ibid.: 2). In Moosonee, Ontario, a two-year nursing diploma course is on-going and geared to a native setting, has a large percentage of students of native ancestry, but is not considered a native nursing programme as such (Irvine, 1987).

The health status of many of Canada's native people (the status Indian, the non-status Indian, the Inuit and the Métis) remains far from satisfactory. The life-expectancy of a status Indian, for example, is much less than that of a non-native person, with high levels of poverty, unemployment and underemployment an everyday reality for many native people (Mardiros, 1987; Rootman, 1988). Mardiros (1987) emphasizes the need to view the health status of native people in its historical context, recognizing the detrimental effects that certain historical factors have had on native health and traditional native ways. Not only have traditional health practices been impotent against many diseases (e.g. smallpox, influenza) introduced by European traders and others, but traditional structures (i.e. social and economic) have been severely undermined by government and other outside agencies. It is only in more recent times that traditional approaches to healing and caring, whether alone or in tandem with western scientific approaches (e.g. Timpson et al., 1988), have been found acceptable to a wider number of health professionals of the western medical tradition. More emphasis is now being placed on native people leading the way as regards the provision of health care services to native people (e.g. Hagey and Buller, 1983; Gregory and Stewart, 1987).

Despite an increasing emphasis on traditional health practices, and the need for more native people in nursing, there is still scant indication that Canadian nursing has considered the value of traditional native healing and caring practices to the non-native client, as dramatized in the film *Dreamspeaker* (CBC, 1977). This film vividly portrays the different approach to care that an Indian healer offers to a non-native boy who has received institutionalized care for fire-raising. The young boy is helped in finding a way through his various personal and social difficulties which western medico-social approaches have failed to achieve. The film challenges the viewer to consider the possibilities, indeed the humanity, that native health care practices hold.

The potential of Indian healing practices for a non-native clientele, in this instance for psoriasis, is also the topic of a paper by Young et al. (1988). While a rigorous scientific research study was not feasible, improvements in client health were effected despite the sense of intrusion that the research study placed on the building of a healing milieu.

Inuit culture, like the various Canadian Indian cultures, has been prey to the incursions of Europeans into Canada's northlands, resulting in cultural disruption and the introduction of infectious diseases. Traditional Inuit culture has its own educational, legal, health and economic structures. Change has made it very difficult for both young and older Inuit to maintain the cultural ways and a sense of Inuit identity. By tradition, the Inuit live close to the land, and land and nature assume immense cultural importance. While many Inuit uphold differing forms of Christianity, and some the Baha'i faith, their traditional religion involves worshipping 'the spirits of nature who protect us' (Ekoomiak, 1988: 23). In Inuit as in native Indian culture, elders should be accorded respect. But, as Inuit life increasingly takes on the ways, expectations and technologies of western society (e.g. computerized technology, western medical care and pharmacopoeia, and university education), the traditions of former years are not always the ways of the young, nor is today's lifestyle always seen as so satisfying. Many Inuit have little access to regular and satisfying wage employment; if they do not enjoy life on the land, they may fail to develop a sense of pride in their heritage (e.g. Anoee, 1979).

UNITED STATES OF AMERICA

Like Canada, the United States is a cultural mix, with certain ethnic groups more numerically prominent than others in differing states, regions and localities (e.g. Blacks and Mexicans are dominant in the southern states). Initially dominated by the Protestant Anglo-American culture established during the colonial era, the United States has since become the homeland for many people from a wide diversity of cultural heritages, a 'micro-world reflecting the cultural diversity of the entire larger world' (Murillo-Rohde, 1976: 26). As in Canada, the indigenous Indian peoples, who comprise various tribal groups such as the Navajo, Sioux and Cherokee, are now cultural minorities.

Earlier expectations of assimilation of minority cultural groups into the dominant culture have not materialized. Though some cultural melting and fusion has taken place, particularly along racial lines, many cultural minorities have resisted becoming part of a pan-American 'melting-pot'. At various times in American history, certain cultural minorities have been considered undesirable and openly excluded from the process of assimilation into the dominant American culture (see Ward, 1982). Indeed, despite constitutional guarantees, various ethnic groups have borne the brunt of varying forms of discrimination, whether because of the predominant religion of their group, or because of their ethnic origins. The Hutterites, for instance, were persecuted for their pacifist views and refusal to wear uniform when drafted for military service during the First World War. Many at this time sought religious freedom in Canada (Dyck, 1981). In 1882, the Exclusion Act placed restrictions on the immigration of Chinese people (e.g. Bullough and Bullough, 1972: 28). This followed a series of virulent attacks launched on Chinese people living in California where they were employed as labourers to help build the railroads.

The Blacks have also faced much hardship. Not only have they endured the cruelty of being wrenched from their homelands in Africa in centuries past to become slaves on the plantations of the South or to work in the homes of the more affluent, but even in modern times they continue to be among the least privileged groups as far as health care, education and housing are concerned. During the early pioneering days, the native Indians were virtually exterminated, either through warfare or by disease introduced by settlers. Government policies in force at different times have sometimes encouraged the integration of Indians into the mainstream of American life, or at other times encouraged them to live on reservations and to preserve the cultural integrity of the tribal unit (Bullough and Bullough, 1972: 96–7). As used for the 1970 census in the USA, the definition of an American Indian is a person who resides on a reservation or whose name appears on a tribal roll. Figures based on this classification can be misleading, for persons of Indian ancestry who no longer lived in their native villages may have been classified as non-Indian, while some with minimal Indian ancestry but who lived on a reservation will have been included (Ruffin, 1979: 5). In the 1980 census, American Indians are again identified from a question on race, but 'regardless of residence' (United States, 1980a: 3).

The character of ethnic and racial diversity in the United States has been tied closely to the country's economic development (Ruffin, 1979: 3). Between the sixteenth and eighteenth centuries, the slave trade was an important economic institution. Although poor Europeans had been imported in the early seventeenth century, it was the black slaves who were used in large numbers to cultivate vast tracts of arable land. Later, during the nineteenth and twentieth centuries, immigrants arrived from many European countries, initially from the north and west and later from countries in eastern and southern Europe. These early pioneers provided the human energy and resources needed to open the western frontiers. Those who followed them often arrived destitute and exhausted after long and gruelling journeys. Though many had worked on farms in their homelands, few moved into rural areas. Instead, they found work in the industrial cities and towns along the eastern seaboard, and in cities, such as Cleveland, Chicago and Buffalo, which were situated along the major railroads. As newcomers, they often took over housing in areas where previous immigrants from other countries had lived, 'Germantowns' becoming Little Italies, and Irish enclaves the homes of Russian Jews (Bullough and Bullough, 1972: 24).

Many ethnic minority groups lived in the urban ghettos which Ward (1982: 376) describes as 'striking geographic manifestations of ethnic pluralism'. The term 'ghetto' was originally used in Venice and thereafter throughout Europe from the Middle Ages onwards in reference to those districts in which Jews were legally confined. Its use in nineteenth-century America, however, is in reference to congested inner-city residential quarters, initially those where Eastern

European Jewish people and later where newly arrived immigrants from many different countries resided. Here immigrants were able to uphold the cultural traditions of their homelands, sharing and perpetuating their traditions with other members of their own ethnic heritage. The ghetto served as a 'decompression chamber', one in which 'familiar faces and customs mediated the immigrants' initial encounter with urban America' (Ward, 1982: 378). Although there were advantages in living in the ghettos, discrimination could easily be levied against one particular racial, ethnic or religious group by both landlords and city services, who could allow housing in specific areas to become grossly dilapidated, and waste collection to be poorly maintained (Bullough and Bullough, 1972: 25).

Reasons for emigration varied. In the nineteenth century, many emigrated from Ireland because of religious and political discrimination, economic hardship and, in the 1840s, to escape famine when potato blight ruined the country's staple foodcrop. For others, emigration was a result of political circumstance in their homeland, and for many Africans, their abduction into the slave trade. Some immigrants saw themselves as sojourners, and, intending to return home, made conscious efforts to keep their culture alive. Others, such as the black slaves, developed new cultural patterns in the process of survival. For instance, as black couples were frequently separated, as a result of being sold by their slave owners, their marriages not being legally recognized, matrifocal households increasingly became the norm, many women having to raise their offspring without the child's father to help. In more recent times, strong kinship and community bonds help many Blacks survive in the face of adversity (e.g. Bloch, 1983: 99–100).

Over the past several decades, mass migration to the United States has been primarily from non-European sources, many such newcomers (e.g. Puerto-Ricans) adding to the numbers of visible ethnic minorities which form contemporary America's pluralist society. At the same time, there has also been a 'rediscovery' of ethnicity, an increase in ethnic consciousness, among 'white ethnics'. It has been suggested that this rediscovery is possibly a means of gaining some measure of power and privilege, perhaps a result of growing scepticism about the 'American Dream', or perhaps from a sense of threat or jealousy, ethnic groups of colour being considered no more deserving of privileges claimed than white ethnics (see Isajiw, 1978: 33).

As a term currently used throughout the United States, 'ethnic groups of colour', embraces Hispanics, Blacks, American Indians and Orientals (Tripp-Reimer, 1986: 208). In addition to 'white', the 1980 US Census (United States, 1980b: 2) identified the following racial categories: Black, American Indian, Eskimo and Aleut, and Asian and Pacific Islander. Different authors use variations of these ethnic/racial groups. Murillo-Rohde (1976: 26), for instance, refers to Native Americans or Indians, Blacks, Spanish-speaking, Asian Americans and Aleuts. Monrroy (1983: 116–18) uses the term 'Raza/Latina' for people living in the United States who may or may not be Spanish-speaking, and whose origins are in Latin America (e.g. Mexican/Chicano, Central American, Cuban, Puerto-Rican and people of South American ancestry). In the United States, the term 'Asian' invariably embraces people from eastern Asia (e.g. Filipinos, Chinese, Korean, Vietnamese and Japanese and also from countries in South Asia), with those from Samoa and Hawaii being known as Pacific Islanders. Indians from the Indian Subcontinent are given the appellation 'Asian Indian', thereby differentiating them from the American or Canadian Indian, the term 'South Asian' not holding the currency in the United States that it does in the United Kingdom.

Within both the racially darker (ethnic people of colour) and the white ethnic groups, there is a wide diversity of cultural groups, and many studies exist which describe the lifestyles of these groups. A growing number of such studies has been, and is being, undertaken by nurses. Many nursing texts and articles are now available to help nurses gain some understanding of the traditions and lifestyles of the various cultural groups in contemporary America, and of how they, as nurses, can provide more culturally relevant nursing care for those people. The following are examples of publications written by nurses which provide insight into the provision of nursing care for clients and patients from various cultures:

Gypsies (Anderson and Tighe, 1973), Arab Americans (Meleis and Sorrell, 1981), Navajo Indians (Satz, 1982), Muckleshoot Indians (Horn, 1979), Greeks (Tripp-Reimer, 1983), Filipinos (Stern, 1981) and Blacks (Bloch, 1983). There seems, however, to be the same general assumption as found in other countries, as to what is the dominant culture. This is seldom spelt out, exceptions being Miner's (1956) parody on the dominant culture of the United States: 'Body ritual among the Nacirema' (that is, the Americans), and a more serious statement by Smoyak (1979: 62–4) entitled 'American Indian nurses can learn about the Great White Majority'. The evolving ways of the dominant culture remain embedded in countless articles and texts – ways which one is somehow supposed to know, the need for explication seemingly not required in the same way as in regard to ethnic minority groups.

OTHER COUNTRIES WORLDWIDE

This section provides a brief overview of various aspects relating to the multicultural composition of countries in Europe, and also to health concerns of the indigenous peoples of Australia and New Zealand. As practically any country could be discussed to some extent in regard to its ethnic composition and the need for culturally-sensitive nursing care, the reader is encouraged to look further in the literature relating to the country of interest. In many countries, the nursing literature is not published in English, thus limiting the access that many nurses have to gaining insight into nursing concerns in such countries. Nevertheless, international journals, such as the *International Nursing Review*, provide the anglophone nurse with useful articles and updates on nursing activities and multicultural concerns worldwide.

Europe

Throughout the centuries, partitions, alliances and wars have regularly changed the map of Europe. The people of

Alsace-Lorraine, for instance, have found themselves at different times first in Germany then in France, having to adjust many times to serial changes in national identity. As a consequence of changing national boundaries, many European countries comprise a number of cultural groups, and indeed, several languages are spoken in many countries. Switzerland, for instance, has four national languages: French, German, Italian and Romansch. The Basque people, a minority group that has maintained its identity over countless centuries, reside in both France and Spain. With distinctly different cultural ways from those of the main populace of the countries they inhabit, the Lapps are found in Sweden, Norway, Finland and the north-west regions of the USSR. Religious dissidents have also been instrumental in introducing new cultural ways to other countries. The French Huguenots, for example, sought refuge in England and Prussia, taking their language and religious ideals with them, not to mention numerous occupational skills (see Reaman, 1963).

Today, the population of the Netherlands includes increasing numbers of ethnic minority groups from former Dutch colonies (e.g. Surinam, Netherlands Antilles), and the population of France includes minorities from her former colonies in Africa such as Morocco, Algeria and Senegal as well as from islands in the French Antilles such as Martinique. During the time of rapid economic expansion in the 1950s and 1960s, waves of labour migration brought many workers, often termed 'guest workers', to countries in north-west Europe. Several European countries, such as France and West Germany, have employed many migrant labourers from Eastern European and Mediterranean countries (e.g. Yugoslavia, Greece, Spain, Turkey). In France, many of these migrant workers settled in Paris, Marseilles and Lyons where employment opportunities were the highest. Living in ghettos, many faced impoverishment, substandard housing and discrimination in regard to social provision, their lot often depending upon prevailing governmental attitudes which have ranged from 'the liberal to the repressive' (Ogden, 1982: 318).

Accidents occurring among industrial migrants in France

have been found to be higher in number than those occurring among indigenous workers (Berger and Mohr, 1975). But how has the French nursing profession responded? As more literature relating to the provision of culturally appropriate nursing, and indeed health-care, in European countries begins to emerge in journals and texts published in English (e.g. Verkleij, 1976; Dawes, 1986; Raya, 1989), so the wealth of experience that European nurses and other European health workers have to offer will be available to a wider number of nurses internationally. However, some insight into nursing as practised in different European countries is needed if our understanding of developments in transcultural nursing in Europe is to be contexturally meaningful (e.g. Quinn, 1980; Sims, 1990). The choice of Maastricht in the Netherlands as the venue for the 1989 annual conference of the North American-based Transcultural Nursing Society (the central theme of the conference being migration) indicates a firm recognition of the important contribution that European nurses have to offer to transcultural nursing worldwide.

New Zealand and Australia

In this section the focus is mainly on the health of the indigenous peoples of Australia and New Zealand. Examples of culture-specific ways that have relevance to health promotion and nursing care are included.

New Zealand

As in North America, early European explorers and settlers brought diseases such as whooping cough, syphilis and tuberculosis to the Maori people of New Zealand. Despite devastating changes to Maori health, and indeed to all aspects of traditional Maori life, during the 200 years following Cook's arrival in 1769, the Maori notion of health has remained surprisingly unchanged. For the Maori, health is an 'integrated view of birth, growth and development, maturity, old age and death' which is closely inter-linked to the Maori relationship with 'the land and the sea and the beings which inhabit those places, inanimate, animate, living and dead' (Ramsden and Erihe, 1988: 2). The Treaty of Waitangi, 1840, between the European settlers and the Maori, included certain guarantees regarding possessions belonging to the chiefs and tribes of New Zealand. One possession treasured by the Maori is their health status which, according to Ramsden and Erihe (1988: 2), is seen as 'a gift from the ancestors to be treasured and held reverently as part of the holistic cycle'.

Today, the Maori form approximately 10 per cent of New Zealand's population and have 'morbidity and mortality rates that are much higher than [those of] the general population' (Quinlan, 1988: 13; also Boddy, 1988). For the most part, New Zealand's health services are shaped by monocultural structures that generally fail to regard Maori people as active partners in the planning and provision of health services. In the eyes of many whose concern is to improve the Maori people's situation, racism needs to be overcome and a true spirit of bi-culturalism between the Maori and the Pakeha (the non-Maori) developed before multiculturalism can ever become a reality (see Abbott, 1987; Ramsden, 1990). Although the need to provide health care services that are in keeping with Maori cultural ways has received increasing recognition in recent years, this part of New Zealand's health service could benefit from further development. One development in the Auckland area is a mental health service for a Maori clientele. Using a Maori cultural framework, this service also accepts non-Maori clients who wish to be cared for in the Maori way (Quinlan, 1988).

Health for the Maori embodies four interrelated components, spiritual (*te taha wairua*), mental or psychic (*te taha hinengaro*), physical (*te taha tinana*) and family/extended kinship system (*te taha whanau*), each component viewed within Maori cultural dimensions (Durie, 1985). Spiritual well-being, which is considered the most basic and fundamental requirement for health, includes religious beliefs but also implies a spiritual communion with the environment. Physical well-being involves separating the sacred from the common, and includes a variety of ritual procedures relating to bodily functions. Cleansing the body and the consumption of food are considered polar opposites. To bring together items for elimination and for consumption in one piece of furniture, such as a hospital bedside locker, is to fail to uphold Maori health values and to undermine the Maori patient's confidence in the health professional (Durie, 1985: 484; also Boddy, 1988).

Various articles are to be found in recent volumes of the *New Zealand Nursing Journal* (also known as the *Kai Tiaki*) which advocate the inclusion of Maori health concepts and culture into New Zealand's nurse education. It is recommended that Maori culture should be taught by Maori elders and Maori nurses. Recognizing the possible strain that this may place on scarce Maori resources, Abbott (1987: 28) suggests that courses for multidisciplinary groups of health professionals might be a more practical solution. Among its aims, the National Council of Maori Nurses seeks to encourage more Maoris to become nurses and to promote the incorporation of Maori values into nurse education. Today, Maori people wish to promote and provide health care services that adhere to Maori cultural ways. Seeing health 'as a part of who they are, where they have come from and where they are going', the Maori 'wish to take responsibility for their own health at the level of *whanau* (extended family), *hapu* (sub-tribe) or *iwi* (tribe) rather than as individuals' (Boddy, 1988: 36).

Australia

With a population of approximately 15 million people, many of whom live in the six capital cities, Australia is a large country with a relatively small population. Providing health care to vast rural areas is a challenge that Australia has responded to, in part, by the formation of the Flying Doctor Service and outback nursing services. Like New Zealand, Australia was originally settled by white Europeans who were predominantly from the United Kingdom, the Aborigine becoming a racial/cultural minority. Today, the population of Australia is unquestionably multi-ethnic (see Burnley, 1982; Clements, 1986). Heffernan (1986: 212) suggests that Australian society is in fact 'moving towards a mixed cultural society rather than a multicultural one as many second generation migrants marry outside their own ethnic group'.

Migration to Australia was at its highest during the gold rushes of the 1850s and again during the years following the Second World War. In more recent times, immigrants have arrived from Asia, Latin America, the Lebanon, Vietnam and, once again, from Europe (Clements, 1986: 9; Heffernan, 1986: 212). While the health concerns of migrant workers (e.g. Italians) have warranted, and have received, serious attention (see Judge, 1977; Koutsounadis, 1977; Idrus, 1988), it is the health needs of the Aborigines that are of immense concern, for substantially poor levels of health are found consistently among the Aboriginal Australians.

Stacey (1974; 1977) and Brandl and Tilley (1981a and b) have been involved in health projects among Aboriginal groups, Stacey in Central Australia and Brandl and Tilley in the Northern Territory. All advocate that nurses should learn how the Aborigine client construes his or her world, and what meanings are ascribed to given situations. Each brings to the forefront how much can be learnt by the nurse, to the benefit of the client, if she or he takes time to understand Aboriginal people's ways.

Stacey points out how one activity may assume different meanings to people from differing cultures. The Aborigine who agrees to be involved in a health education project may do so because he or she places high regard on interaction with other people. For the Aborigine, actions are 'performed to express or consolidate relationships' (Stacey, 1977: 36). The European-Australian health worker, however, is more likely to be interested in building a relationship with the Aborigine client in order to teach some aspect of health rather than as a relationship, an interaction, in itself. Indeed, ideas and values that Aborigines

hold dear and adhere to contrast profoundly with those of European-Australians. . . . Aborigines. . . are an intensely spiritual people who have developed the skills and organisation of social relationships to a very sophisticated degree. Their emphases are kinship and religion. (Brandl and Tilley, 1981b: 7)

Approaches to health promotion and health concerns also assume cultural dimensions. To the Aborigines Stacey (1977: 37) worked with, 'preventive health' measures may include ensuring that a child wears shoes to prevent a spirit entering the child's footprint and causing sickness. Yet, a European-Australian health worker might wonder why a family with little money would buy shoes rather than nourishing food. For the Aborigines that Brandl and Tilley (1981a: 26; 1981b: 16–17) write about, teaching involves reinforcing correct behaviour and, if possible, ignoring mistakes. The social cost of making a mistake is considered greater than that of admitting ignorance. Successful accomplishment, however, requires praise. By being aware of culture-specific styles of learning, nurses are better able to promote health in ways that are more culturally acceptable and comfortable to Aborigine people. Thus, cultural insight and knowledge become essential prerequisites to effective, client-centred nursing practice.

REFERENCES

Introduction

Auld MG (1979) Nursing in a changing society. *Journal of Advanced Nursing* 4(3): 287–98.

Cottle T (1977) A wasted death? *New Society* 41(782): 656–7.

Driedger L (1978) Introduction. Ethnic identity in the Canadian mosaic. In L Driedger (ed.), *The Canadian Ethnic Mosaic. A quest for identity.* Toronto: McClelland & Stewart.

ICN (International Council of Nurses) (1973) *Code for Nurses. Ethical concepts applied to nursing.* Geneva: ICN.

Leininger M (1967) The culture concept and its relevance to nursing. *Journal of Nursing Education* 6(2): 27–37.

UKCC (United Kingdom Central Council for Nursing, Midwifery and Health Visiting) (1984) *Code of Professional Conduct for the Nurse, Midwife and Health Visitor*, 2nd edn. London: UKCC.

United Kingdom

Agbolegbe G (1984) Fighting the racist disease. *Nursing Times* 80(16): 18–20.

Anwar M (1979) *The Myth of Return. Pakistanis in Britain.* London: Heinemann.

Ballard R (1972) Family organisation among the Sikhs in Britain. *New Community* **2**(1): 12–24.

Ballard R and Ballard C (1977) The Sikhs: The development of South Asian settlements in Britain. In J L Watson (ed.), *Between Two Cultures*. Oxford: Basil Blackwell.

Brent Community Health Council (1981) *Black People and the Health Service*. London: Brent Community Health Council.

Brown J (1970) *The Un-melting Pot. An English town and its immigrants*. London: Macmillan.

Bryant GM, Davies KJ and Newcombe RG (1979) Standardisation of the Denver Developmental Screening Test for Cardiff Children. *Developmental Medicine and Child Neurology* **21**(3): 353–64.

Constantinides P (1977) The Greek Cypriots. Factors in the maintenance of ethnic identity. In JL Watson (ed.), *Between Two Cultures*. Oxford: Basil Blackwell.

Eyles J (1982) Black and British. *The Geographical Magazine* **54**(5): 277–83.

File N and Power C (1981) *Black Settlers in Britain. 1555–1958*. Oxford: Heinemann Educational Books.

Fink KP (1979) Victims of political–racial persecution. *Nursing Times* **75**(12): 496–9.

Ghuman PAS (1980) *Bhattra* Sikhs in Cardiff: family and kinship organisation. *New Community* **8**(3): 308–16.

Gordon JE (1975) Mary Seacole. A forgotten nurse heroine of the Crimea. *Midwife, Health Visitor and Community Nurse* **11**: 47–50.

Hahlo KG (1980) Profile of a Gujarati community in Bolton. *New Community* **8**(3): 295–307.

Jackson B and Garvey A (1974) The Chinese children of Britain. *New Society* **30**(626): 9–12.

Jones HR and Davenport M (1972) The Pakistani community in Dundee. *Scottish Geographical Magazine* **88**(2): 75–85.

Mares P (1982) *The Vietnamese in Britain. A handbook for health workers*. Cambridge: Health Education Council/National Extension College.

Okely J (1983) *The Traveller-Gypsies*. Cambridge: Cambridge University Press.

Open University (1982) *Bedford: Portrait of a multi-ethnic town*. Course text for Ethnic Minorities and Community Relations prepared by R Jeffcoate and B Mayor. Milton Keynes: Open University Press.

Pearson M (1987) Racism. The great divide. *Nursing Times* **83**(24): 24–6.

Philpott SB (1977) The Montserratians: Migration dependency and the maintenance of island ties in England. In JL Watson (ed.), *Between Two Cultures*. Oxford: Basil Blackwell.

Rack PH (1978) Stress among immigrants. *Stress Today* [publication by CIBA], December: 1, 4–5.

Rousseau N (1983) Give us a playpiece, please; not lectures! *Journal of the Royal Society of Health* **103**(3): 104–11.

Saifullah Khan V (1977) The Pakistanis: Mirpuri villagers at home and in Bradford. In JL Watson (ed.), *Between Two Cultures*. Oxford: Basil Blackwell.

Salter J (1873) *The Asiatic in England*. London: Seeley, Jackson & Halliday.

Torkington P (1987) Sorry, wrong colour. *Nursing Times* **83**(24): 27–8.

UKCC (United Kingdom Central Council for Nursing, Midwifery and Health Visiting) (1984) *Code of Professional Conduct for the Nurse, Midwife and Health Visitor*, 2nd edn. London: UKCC.

United Kingdom Laws, Statutes, etc. (1905) *Aliens Act*. 5 Edward 7, ch. 13.

Watson JL (1977) The Chinese: Hong Kong villagers in the British catering trade. In JL Watson (ed.), *Between Two Cultures*. Oxford: Basil Blackwell.

Canada

Anderson JM (1985) Perspectives on the health of immigrant women. A feminist analysis. *Advances in Nursing Science* **8**(1): 61–76.

Anoee MP (1979) Remembered childhood. In *Ajurnarmat*, Special edition: The Education. Issue No. 4. Eskimo Point, NWT: Inuit Cultural Institute.

Canada, House of Commons (1988) *Bill C–93. Canadian Multiculturalism Act*. 2nd Session. 33rd Parliament. 35–36–37. Elizabeth 2.

Cardenas B and Lucarz J (1985) Canadian Indian health care: A model for service. In M Stewart, J Innes, S Searl and C Smillie (eds), *Community Health Nursing in Canada*. Toronto: Gage.

CBC (Canadian Broadcasting Corporation) (1977) *Dreamspeaker*. [Television film]. Director: C Jutra. Canadian Broadcasting Corporation.

CBC (Canadian Broadcasting Corporation) (1981) *The Golden Mountain. The Chinese in Canada.* [Television film]. Producer/ Director: T Macartney-Filgate.

Drakulic L and Tanaka W (1981) The East Indian family in Canada. *The Canadian Nurse* **77**(3): 24–6.

Dyck CJ (ed.) (1981) *An Introduction to Mennonite History*, 2nd edn. Kitchener, ON: Herald Press.

Ekoomiak N (1988) *Arctic Memories.* Toronto: NC Press.

England J (1986) Cross-cultural health care. *Canada's Mental Health* **34**(4): 13–15.

Gibbon JM (1947) *Three Centuries of Canadian Nursing.* Toronto: Macmillan.

Gregory D and Stewart P (1987) Nurses and traditional healers. Now is the time to speak. *The Canadian Nurse*, **83**(8): 25–7.

Hagey R and Buller E (1983) Drumming and dancing. A new rhythm in nursing care. *The Canadian Nurse* **79**(4): 28–31.

Health and Welfare, Canada (1986) *Achieving Health for All. A framework for health promotion.* Ottawa: Health and Welfare, Canada.

IINC (Indian and Inuit Nurses of Canada) (n.d., c. 1985) *10th Anniversary. The story of the Indian and Inuit nurses of Canada.* Ottawa: IINC.

Irvine R (1987) Nursing education moves to the north. *The Canadian Nurse* **83**(2): 16–18.

Kendall PRW (1983) Prenatal educational programming for Hindi, Punjabi, and Cantonese speaking communities. *Canadian Journal of Public Health* **74**(6): 434–8.

Kulig J (1988a) Childbearing Cambodian refugee women. *The Canadian Nurse* **84**(6): 46–7.

Kulig JC (1988b) Conception and birth control use: Cambodian refugee women's beliefs and practices. *Journal of Community Health Nursing* **5**(4): 235–46.

Leininger M (ed.) (1978) *Transcultural Nursing. Concepts, theories, and practices.* New York: John Wiley.

Mardiros M (1987) Primary health care and Canada's indigenous people. *The Canadian Nurse* **83**(8): 20–4.

Orque MS (1983) Orque's ethnic/cultural system. A framework for ethnic nursing care. In MS Orque, B Bloch and LSA Monrroy (eds), *Ethnic Nursing Care. A multicultural approach.* St Louis: CV Mosby.

Richmond AH (1969) Immigration and pluralism in Canada. *International Migration Review* **5**: 5–24.

Rootman I (1988) Inequities in health: sources and solutions.

Health Promotion. Winter: 2–8.

Timpson J, McKay S, Kakegamic S, Roundhead D, Cohen C and Matewapit G (1988) Depression in a native Canadian in northwestern Ontario: Sadness, grief or spiritual illness? *Canada's Mental Health* 36(2/3): 5–8.

Waxler-Morrison N, Anderson JM and Richardson E (eds) (1990) *Cross-cultural Caring: a handbook for health professionals in western Canada.* Vancouver: University of British Columbia Press.

Yoshida M and Davies M (1985) An innovative project. Childbearing and childrearing. Recent immigrant families in the urban Toronto setting. In M Stewart, J Innes, S Searl and C Smillie (eds), *Community Health Nursing in Canada.* Toronto: Gage.

Young DE, Morse JM, Swartz L and Ingram G (1988) The Psoriasis Research Project. An overview. In DE Young (ed.), *Health Care Issues in the Canadian North.* Edmonton, AB: Boreal Institute for Northern Studies.

United States of America

Anderson G and Tighe B (1973) Gypsy culture and health care. *American Journal of Nursing* 73(2): 282–5.

Bloch B (1983) Nursing care of black patients. In MS Orque, B Bloch and LSA Monrroy (eds), *Ethnic Nursing Care. A multicultural approach.* St Louis: CV Mosby.

Bullough B and Bullough VL (1972) *Poverty, Ethnic Identity, and Health Care.* New York: Appleton-Century-Crofts.

Dyck CJ (ed.) (1981) *An Introduction to Mennonite History,* 2nd edn. Kitchener, ON: Herald Press.

Horn BM (1979) Transcultural nursing and child-rearing of the Muckleshoot people. In M Leininger (ed.), *Transcultural Nursing '79.* New York: Masson.

Isajiw WW (1978) Olga in Wonderland: Ethnicity in a technological society. In L Driedger (ed.), *The Canadian Ethnic Mosaic. A quest for identity.* Toronto: McClelland & Stewart.

Meleis AI and Sorrell L (1981) Arab American women and their birth experiences. *MCN [American Journal of Maternal/Child Nursing]* 6(3): 171–6.

Miner H (1956) Body ritual among the Nacirema. *American Anthropologist* 58(3): 503–7.

Monrroy LSA (1983) Nursing care of Raza/Latina patients. In MS Orque, B Bloch and LSA Monrroy (eds), *Ethnic Nursing Care. A multicultural approach.* St Louis: CV Mosby.

Murillo-Rohde I (1976) Unique needs of ethnic minority clients in a multiracial society. A socio-cultural perspective. In *Affirmative Action. Toward quality nursing care for a multiracial society.* Kansas City, MO: American Nurses' Association.

Ruffin JE (1979) Changing perspectives on ethnicity and health. In *A Strategy for Change.* Papers presented at a conference held on 9–10 June, by the American Nurses' Association Commission on Human Rights at Albuquerque, NM [Kansas City, MO: ANA].

Satz KJ (1982) Integrating Navajo tradition into maternal–child nursing. *Image* 14(3): 89–91.

Smoyak SA (1979) Nurse and client ethnicity and its effects upon interaction. In *A Strategy for Change.* Papers presented at a conference held on 9–10 June, by the American Nurses' Association Commission on Human Rights at Albuquerque, NM [Kansas City, MO: ANA].

Stern PN (1981) Solving problems of cross-cultural health teaching. The Filipino childbearing family. *Image* 13(2): 47–50.

Tripp-Reimer T (1983) Retention of a folk-healing practice (*Matiasma*) among four generations of urban Greek immigrants. *Nursing Research* 32(2): 97–101.

Tripp-Reimer T (1986) Health heritage project. A research proposal submitted to the division of nursing. *Western Journal of Nursing Research* 8(2): 207–28.

United States (US Department of Commerce, Bureau of the Census) (1980a) *American Indians and the 1980 Census.* US Government Publications No. 80–9522. Washington, DC.

United States (US Department of Commerce, Bureau of the Census) (1980b) *1980 Census of the Population. Age, sex, race, and Spanish origin of the population by regions, divisions, and states* (Supplementary report). US Government Publications No. PC80–S1–1. Washington, DC.

Ward D (1982) The North American ghetto. *The Geographical Magazine* 54(7): 376–80.

Other Countries Worldwide

Europe

Berger J and Mohr J (1975) '*A Seventh Man*'. *The story of a migrant worker in Europe.* Harmondsworth: Penguin Books.

Dawes T (1986) Multicultural nursing. *International Nursing Review* 33(5): 148–50.

Ogden P (1982) France adapts to immigration with difficulty. *The Geographical Magazine* 54(6): 318–23.

Quinn S (ed.) (1980) *Nursing in the European Community*. London: Croom Helm.

Raya A (1989) Family care of the elderly in Greece: Culture and research. In CA Dye (ed.), *Recent Advances in Nursing* [Nursing elderly people] **23**: 72–81.

Reaman GE (1963) *The Trail of the Huguenots*. Toronto: Allen.

Sims J (1990) Nursing in Spain. Times of change. *Nursing Times* **86**(12): 30–1.

Verkleij H (1976) Gonorrhoea and foreign immigrants at Rotterdam University Hospital. *British Journal of Venereal Diseases*, **52**: 84–7.

New Zealand

Abbott M (1987) Taha Maori in comprehensive nursing education. *NZ Nursing Journal* **81**(10): 27–9.

Boddy JM (1988) Maori health – is the future determined by the past? In J M Morse (ed.), *Recent Advances in Nursing* [Issues in cross-cultural nursing], **20**. Edinburgh: Churchill Livingstone.

Durie MH (1985) A Maori perspective of health. *Social Science and Medicine* **20**(5): 483–6.

Quinlan J (1988) Radicals, racism and revolution? *NZ Nursing Journal* **81**(7): 13–14.

Ramsden I (1990) *Piri ki nga tangaroa*. In anticipation of better days. *NZ Nursing Journal* **83**(1): 16–18.

Ramsden I and Erihe L (1988) 'Our culture is our health' (Editorial). *NZ Nursing Journal*, **81**(7): 2–3.

Australia

Brandl M and Tilley E (1981a) Marching to a different drum. *The Australasian Nurses' Journal* **10**(9): 24–31.

Brandl M and Tilley E (1981b) *Marching to a Different Drum*. Centre for Resource and Environmental Studies, Australian National University: Canberra.

Burnley IH (1982) Where the British are immigrants. *The Geographical Magazine* **54**(10): 560–3.

Clements A (1986) Demography and statistics. In A Clements (ed.), *Infant and Family Health in Australia*. Melbourne: Churchill Livingstone.

Heffernan A (1986) The needs of multiethnic families. In A Clements (ed.), *Infant and Family Health in Australia*. Melbourne: Churchill Livingstone.

Idrus L (1988) Transcultural nursing in Australia. Response to a changing population base. In JM Morse (ed.), *Recent Advances in Nursing* [Issues in cross-cultural nursing], **20**. Edinburgh: Churchill Livingstone.

Judge S (1977) Some social aspects of illness among Italian migrants. *The Australian Nurses' Journal* **6**(12): 41–3.

Koutsounadis V (1977) The migrant child in the hospital and health care system. *Australasian Nurses Journal* **6**(11): 20–2.

Stacey S (1974) Cultures in collision. *Australasian Nurses Journal* **2**(38): 12.

Stacey S (1977) What do we mean by subjective data? An analysis of a health education programme in Alice Springs. *The Australian Nurses' Journal* **6**(8): 34–8.

CHAPTER 2

Nursing, Health and Culture

In the previous chapter we considered the multicultural composition of various countries where nursing is practised at a professional level. Although cultural norms shape the way we think, feel and act, many of us seldom consider the extent to which we are culture-bound. Health beliefs and practices are among the many cultural traditions we inherit socially. As these vary from culture to culture, it is important that nurses who work with multicultural clienteles are proficient in discovering and using cultural information so that they can better provide culturally-sensitive and appropriate nursing care and promote health that is truly client-oriented.

In the first part of this chapter, three topics will be discussed: these are nursing, health and culture. Nursing and health will be considered both in general terms and specifically in regard to cultural factors. Thereafter, all three topics will be linked, and various aspects of the cultural dimension to nursing considered. Rather than viewing culturally-sensitive nursing practice as a nicety to be achieved when time permits, it is hoped that the reader will appreciate the importance of culture to effective nursing care and feel keen to promote at practical, educational, research and administrative levels of nursing, approaches to care that are meaningful to the client in the context of the client's culture.

NURSING

Much time and energy has been directed by nurse theorists and others towards defining what 'nursing is'. And there are many definitions. From these Donaldson and Crowley (1978: 113) have distilled three general themes which sum up 'the essence or core of nursing':

1. 'Concern with principles and laws that govern the life processes, well-being, and optimum functioning of human beings–sick or well' (see e.g. Nightingale, 1860; Rogers, 1970).
2. 'Concern with the patterning of human behavior in interaction with the environment in critical life situations' (see e.g. Johnson, 1961; Rogers, 1970).
3. 'Concern with the processes by which positive changes in health status are affected' (see e.g. Peplau, 1952; Leininger, 1981).

In more basic terms, Florence Nightingale (1860: 3), in her *Notes on Nursing*, equated nursing with having 'charge of the personal health of somebody'. To have 'charge of' is to be entrusted with, or to take care of, something or someone. Clients and patients entrust nurses with intimate personal knowledge, often with their very selves, in the implicit understanding that nursing has society's assent to promote health and healing to the betterment of the individual and of humankind. Nursing involves a commitment to be caringly involved in the lives of others with the intent of promoting health and healing, and, for those who are dying, a peaceful end.

But the promotion of health and healing does not occur in a vacuum. The environment – which includes all the conditions, circumstances and influences that surround and affect the patient or client (see Roy and Roberts, 1981: 4) – is an important element in the promotion, and indeed in the restoration and maintenance, of health. For the hospitalized patient, the physical and social environments assume particular importance. The design of the hospital ward, for instance, helps shape the extent to which sufficient privacy, acceptable noise levels, appropriate lighting and adequate opportunities for social interaction with other people exist, each aspect being conducive in some measure to the provision of a healing and health-promoting milieu (e.g. Tatton-Brown, 1978). But what is usual in hospitals in one country may be very unusual in another. In India, for instance, it is customary for hospital patients to have a relative remain with them throughout their stay (e.g. Taylor and Cooper, 1972). This, however, is unusual in British hospitals, even when wards are short-staffed, unless the patient is extremely ill or a minor.

The foreign patient, who perhaps is on vacation or works on a cargo vessel sailing in international waters, may become extremely bewildered coping with a set of cultural norms different from those to which he or she is accustomed, be they related to sanitary arrangements, diet or forms of communication. Culturally inappropriate nursing care only adds to the patient finding the hospital environment alien and disturbing (e.g. Lennon, 1974; Kubricht and Clark, 1982). Bhanumathi (1977), who looked at nurses' conceptions of 'sick role' and 'good patient' behaviour in India and the United States, points out how different the expectations of American nurses can be from those held by Indian nurses. Based on the findings of her study, she writes:

> The American cultural emphasis is on independence, self-help, interpersonal relations, and individual sensitivity and Indian cultural beliefs on interdependence, destiny, fatalism, punishment for past sins, and passivity. (Bhanumathi, 1977: 23)

Etymologically, the verb 'to nurse' is derived from the Latin 'to nourish'. In its metaphorical sense, nourishment may also be emotional or spiritual 'food', which contributes in some way to the promotion of health, recovery from illness or a more peaceful death. To nourish implies a sense of giving, a cherishing, a caring. Though caring is central to nursing and indeed it is commonplace to speak about 'nursing care', only a few nurse scholars (notably, Watson, 1979; Leininger, 1981; Colliere, 1986; Benner and Wrubel, 1989) have addressed and explored in depth the concept of 'care'. Ardent in promoting the need for nursing 'care' to become a more clearly explicated concept, Leininger (1981:

9), who considers human care/caring to be the very essence of nursing, provides the following definition. In its generic sense, care refers to: 'those assistive, supportive, or facilitative acts toward or for another individual or group with evident or anticipated needs to ameliorate or improve a human condition or lifeway.' Although human caring is a universal phenomenon, its expressions, processes and patterns vary from culture to culture (ibid.: 11). If nursing care is to be client-oriented, then it too should vary, whenever feasible, with the client's cultural needs and ways.

Through the provision of nursing care – whether in hospital, industry, school, clinic, the home or any other location – nurses aim to help improve the condition of the individual. Nursing care involves being skilled in instrumental techniques (such as changing dressings or giving injections), but it also involves understanding how a patient or client feels, which in intercultural situations requires a willingness to look at life from a different cultural stance. It is important, for example, that a nurse, for whom weeping is culturally acceptable, be alert and sensitive to the needs of someone who weeps within but for whom it is culturally unacceptable to weep openly (see Lipe, 1980). It is also important that a nurse recognizes concerns that a Pakistani Muslim patient with an abdominal stoma may have, since the location of the stoma may cause much distress if sited below the umbilicus and if the patient has difficulty bowing towards Mecca when making the *namaz*, the daily prayers that follow a very formal sequence of actions (see Whitethread, 1981).

In intercultural situations, nursing care should be as congruent as possible with the client's cultural orientation. This involves the nurse being alert to how individual clients view themselves in relationship to others in their social group. In many western societies, nursing focuses on the needs of the individual person (e.g. self-actualization). Whether viewed as the sum of various parts (e.g. social, psychological, biological and spiritual) or as a 'whole person' who is other than, and different from, the sum of the parts, the individual is usually considered distinct from his/her social group. In various other cultures, however, the individual is seen as an integral part of, rather than distinct from, the social group (e.g. family, community) to which they belong. The Samoan view of health, for instance, 'is so interwoven with the predicament of the social group that it is almost inseparable' (Kerslake, 1988: 21). Because 'the illness of a member within the *aiga* [extended family] affects the *aiga* well-being', so family members work together as a group 'to restore the health of their sick relative', older members praying, others constantly watching over the sick person, while yet others prepare the food (ibid.). The importance of the social group to health promotion is also a feature of traditional Fijian culture, the care of the pregnant woman, for example, being 'a community concern and the responsibility of all' (Morse, 1984: 289). Concerned that the foetus should be protected from malevolent forces such as the evil eye, 'the other women of the tribe . . . accompany the expectant mother whenever she leaves the house' (ibid.).

Many cultural factors impinge on the health and well-being of a person, and a nurse cannot be expected to know another culture in great depth, unless they have had the opportunity to become familiar with a particular culture over a period of time. Nor can a patient or client be expected to communicate everything that is culturally important to their nursing care, for most of us seldom think through what we take for granted within our culture, until we are confronted with situations which leave us unsettled or bewildered.

It may also be difficult for patients to let nurses know when they feel culturally distressed by the care they receive. In his account of a stay in a New York hospital, Tao-Kim-Hai (1965) describes how it was only after a verbal outburst on his part that his care began to accord with his expectations. However, public outbursts are unacceptable in Vietnamese culture, so he was left feeling full of guilt for having lost 'face'.

Nurses have many opportunities to encourage patients and clients to discuss their feelings, experiences and preferences. During the initial assessment, and then little by little, nurses can learn about their client's culture: perhaps what nutritional beliefs and practices are important, special factors relating to family and kinship, whether specific hygienic practices are maintained, what symbolic meanings are linked to spatial distances, and in what ways suffering and pain are usually expressed. It can also be helpful to turn to the non-professional as well as the professional literature to gain insight and ideas about a patient's culture. Novels, for example, can provide vivid insights into life as lived in various cultures. The most important information, however, is that provided by the client and those who know the client well, their family and close friends. For, if nursing care is to be truly client-oriented, then it must be relevant not only to the client's culture, but as the client sees this to be.

HEALTH

Since the days of Florence Nightingale, health has been considered one of the concepts central to nursing (see Fawcett, 1984: 5). Indeed, in its various forms and specialities, nursing is concerned, directly or indirectly, with client health. All four principles of health visiting (CETHV, 1977: 9), for instance, focus clearly on the notion of health and health needs:

• The search for health needs,
• The stimulation of the awareness of health needs,
• The influence on policies affecting health,
• The facilitation of health-enhancing activities.

Nurses should therefore give careful thought to the various meanings of 'health', and in their practice take time to discover how the client defines health, what value he, she or it (e.g. family-as-client) places on health and in what circumstances this might vary.

But what is meant by 'health'? Derived from the Middle English word *helthe* and the Old English *hǣlo* meaning 'wholeness' (Jago, 1975: 2), the concept of health has been variously defined (see Keller, 1981). For some, health is 'a state of being' (e.g. WHO definition), while for others it is a 'process of becoming', that is, 'a movement from potentiality to actuality in all aspects of being, physical, emotional, social, intellectual and spiritual' (CETHV, 1977: 21). Despite numerous attempts at clarifying its meaning, health remains conceptually ambiguous. Health may be viewed as 'a commodity', as 'a particular ideal state' or as 'a variable state which enables a person to function normally'. It may also be viewed as 'a reserve of strength', 'an ability to adapt to changing circumstances' or even as 'a resilient spirit' (Seedhouse, 1986: 1). There are many definitions, from which Smith (1981) presents four models, or 'standards', of health, and which Brubaker (1983: 3) lists as:

1. the eudaemonistic model, in which health is self-actualization;
2. the adaptive model, in which health is flexible adaptation to the environment;
3. the role-performance model, in which health is viewed as the ability to carry out social roles;
4. the clinical model, in which health is the absence of signs and symptoms of disease or disability.

According to the theoretical framework used, one person may be deemed healthy and unhealthy at any given moment in time. For example, a woman who has developed severe contractures following a mastectomy may be considered functionally disabled, yet, because her husband feels much more needed than he has hitherto felt, their marriage may be more secure and, because of this, she has become a much happier person (see Sigman, 1979: 88). Notions of 'wellness' and of 'fullness of life' have added to the already varied and numerous conceptual dimensions of health (see Dunn, 1959; Winstead-Fry, 1980; Brubaker, 1983). In general, a wellness lifestyle is one that focuses on reducing the risk of illness and increasing life satisfaction and serenity (Payne, 1983: 394).

Despite the different definitions of 'health', we speak of 'health for all'. Indeed, we frequently hear or read about 'health for all by the year 2000' as being a major challenge for all health workers, nurses included. But should the word 'health' be used in such global terms? On the surface, the concept of health, like that of 'justice', might seem to many to be clear enough. But justice born of one cultural milieu may appear as injustice in different cultural circumstances (e.g. Sissons, 1968). Health is also culturally relative. What constitutes health in one culture may be vastly different from how it is viewed within another culture. The Cree of Canada, for instance, view health as a state of harmony which embraces mind, spirit and body (Cardenas and Lucarz, 1985: 248), while for the Chinese, health within the Taoist tradition involves a balance within the human body of two opposite forces or energies called *yin* and *yang* (Mares, 1982: 47).

If health takes on different meanings in different cultures, what then is meant by 'health for all'? In 1981, as Director-General of the World Health Organization, Mahler (1981: 6) stated:

> 'Health for all' means that health is to be brought within reach of everyone in a given country. And by 'health' is meant a personal state of well-being, not just the availability of health services – a state of health that enables a person to lead a socially and economically productive life. 'Health for all' implies the removal of the obstacles to health – that is to say, the elimination of malnutrition, ignorance, contaminated drinking-water, and unhygienic housing – quite as much as it does the solution of purely medical problems such as a lack of doctors, hospital beds, drugs and vaccines.

While Mahler is defining health as linked to the individual person, and upholding the notion of health as a state of being (also WHO, 1978: 2), the point is clearly made that the health of the individual is influenced by numerous factors within the wider environment. To promote health for the individual or for the group is to be concerned about all aspects of life and living, and to be aware of social, economic, racial and political as well as cultural determinants.

Health has been described as having many faces (Billington, 1978), appropriate technology for health being as concerned with methods of agriculture as it is with ensuring that live vaccines are transported in a viable condition. Health then is shaped to some extent by the circumstances in which the person lives, and the promotion of health involves individuals having access to appropriate and adequate resources to help counteract negative circumstances, so allowing them to develop healthier lifestyles and achieve a greater sense of well-being. But such resources must be relevant to the client's perceived needs. The perceived nutritional needs of a group of single mothers in Toronto (Labonte, 1989), for example, did not include receiving tuition about daily nutrient intakes recommended in Canada's Food Guide (e.g. Health and Welfare Canada, 1988). Instead, they were about finding ways to get nutritious foods at prices the mothers could afford. For these women and their children the promotion of health involved cultivating community gardens, pick-your-own food trips to the countryside and community dinners.

Far from being a Third World phenomenon, multiple deprivation is present amid the affluence of many western countries, affecting the health and quality of countless lives. During the 1970s, for instance, many families in a multiply-deprived part of western Scotland were living in 'foul-smelling house[s] with black fungus on the walls' (Hubley, 1979: 10). For these people, dampness was 'more than merely wet patches on a wall'. Though not life-threatening, it was nevertheless a 'soul-destroying' condition. In the 1940s, it was hoped that a welfare state would abolish the five giants that William Beveridge (Social Insurance and Allied Services, 1942) identified: disease, want, ignorance, squalor and idleness. Although it is now forty years and more since the inception of the National Health Service in Britain, serious inequalities in health (e.g. in regard to racial minorities) continue (see DHSS, 1980; Brent Community Health Council, 1981).

Britain is not alone: 'inequities in health', including those related to ethnicity, are a concern that Canada seeks to reduce, '*Achieving health for all*' being the clarion call for the remainder of this century in Canadian health care (Health and Welfare Canada, 1986; Rootman, 1988). Situations of gross poverty and inadequate nursing care services such as those described by Higgins and Lewin (1971) among Black American families in the Delta Region in Mississippi during the late 1960s, remind us yet again of the immense variations in living conditions that can, and do, exist in affluent nations.

One factor that emerges throughout the literature is the

need for health care to be relevant to the client's culture. Paul (1955: 1), an anthropologist writing on public reactions to health care programmes in various countries, suggests that to help a community improve its health (and one might substitute family, either nuclear or extended, for community), it is important to

> learn to think like the people of that community. Before asking a group of people to assume new health habits, it is wise to ascertain the existing habits, how these habits are linked to one another, what functions they perform, and what they mean to those who practice them.

Nevertheless, to know about a client's cultural beliefs and practices is not enough. It is also important to be able to accept other cultural beliefs and practices as meaningful to members of the particular culture from which they emanate. While it is often the differences between cultures that one notices, at least initially, similarities invariably exist and can provide common ground on which client and nurse can establish a basis for mutual understanding and trust.

CULTURE

When we speak of 'culture' we frequently mean a knowledge and an appreciation of the fine arts, or else the ability to use certain forms of social behaviour at the appropriate time (Temple and Henderson, 1978: 932). However, when we speak of multicultural societies, of health beliefs and practices being culturally defined and of culturally sensitive nursing care, we mean something different. We are referring to the way of life of a society or a group of people.

Although a basic understanding of the concept of culture is often assumed, the concept of 'culture', like that of 'health' and 'nursing', may be defined in different ways. Various writers, notably anthropologists, have provided a variety of definitions and insights into the meaning of culture. Indeed, since Tylor's (1871: 1) classic definition of culture as 'that complex whole which includes knowledge, belief, art, morals, law, custom, and any other capabilities and habits acquired by man as a member of society', 'culture', as an

anthropological concept, 'has undergone many transforma-
tions and there is no present-day consensus about how the
term should be used' (Leach, 1982: 39). Eliot (1948: 41), for
instance, describes culture as 'a way of life' which is more
than the mere 'sum of several activities'. Lewis (1976: 17)
underlines the dynamic complexity and socially inherited
nature of the concept, emphasizing that, 'subject to the
vagaries of innovation and change', culture is passed on 'in a
recognizable form from generation to generation'. In
another definition, culture is viewed as 'an abstraction from
the body of learned behaviour which a group of people, who
share the same tradition, transmit entire to their children'
(Mead, 1953: 9). Culture encompasses both the overarching
institutions of a society and 'the small intimate habits of
daily life, such as the way of preparing or eating food, or of
hushing a child to sleep' (ibid.: 10).

Fig. 6   A Pakistani woman boiling water

Spradley (1979: 5) provides a more processual definition by
defining culture as 'the acquired knowledge that people use
to interpret experience and generate social behavior'. In

similar vein, Frake (1977: 7; also in Spradley, 1979: 7) offers a navigational analogy, seeing culture not as providing 'a cognitive map, but rather a set of principles for map-making and navigation'. 'Different cultures are like different schools of navigation designed to cope with different terrains and seas.' Cast out 'into the imperfectly charted, continually shifting seas of everyday life', 'people are not just map-readers; they are map-makers' (Frake, 1977: 6–7). In these definitions of culture, the emphasis is placed on the insider's rather than the outsider's point of view, in other words, how members of the culture see and interpret their world rather than the view of an outside observer.

An American nurse-anthropologist, Leininger (1978: 491), offers the following definition:

> Culture is the learned and transmitted knowledge about a particular culture with its values, beliefs, rules of behavior, and life-style practices that guides a designated group in their thinking and actions in patterned ways.

Helman (1985: 2), a British medical anthropologist, provides an alternative definition, culture being

> a set of guidelines (both explicit and implicit) which an individual inherits as a member of a particular society, and which tells him how to *view* the world, and how to *behave* in it in relation to other people, to supernatural forces or gods, and to the natural environment. It also provides him with a way of transmitting these guidelines to the next generation – by the use of symbols, language, art and ritual.

Nurses, especially those who visit clients in their homes, have numerous opportunities, in discussions and by observation as well as participation in shared activities, to gain insight into the client's cultural world. The nurse is thus in a position to learn about the cultural health beliefs and practices that the client holds, and so be better able to offer care that is sensitive and relevant to the client's culture.

Each one of us has been socialized into viewing our world in a certain way, the contours of which are culture-specific. All of us are ethnocentric to some degree, seeing our world as embodying all that is right and 'natural' to do and not thinking that others see their world in similar terms. We see what our culture permits us to see, and we find it difficult to imagine life any other way. Whether people from different cultures live in one locality or are geographically far removed from one another, life viewed through one cultural lens can appear vastly different from life through a different cultural lens, just as a map of the world that highlights the land masses and their mountain ranges look vastly different from one that depicts the oceans and their depths or shows levels of precipitation worldwide.

When we first come into contact with a culture that differs from our own, we often notice isolated customs – perhaps wearing the *chador* (Muslim veil) as an everyday practice – and we fail to look at the wider cultural whole of which the individual custom is but a part. Yet to view a detail of culture in isolation from the overall culture in which it is rooted makes it become almost as meaningless as an isolated letter of the alphabet (Leach, 1976: 1). It is not always obvious to an outsider how customs are interlinked, nor the value system that subsumes them. Hence, when promoting health, it is important that nurses consider the wider cultural whole, for people

> cling to a particular practice or belief not merely because it is familiar and traditional but because it is linked to other elements of the culture. Conversely, a change effected in one area of the culture may bring with it unexpected changes in other areas. (Paul, 1958: 1503)

In parts of rural India, for example, going to the open fields to defecate used to provide women with the opportunity to gather together to exchange news and take a welcome break from their domestic routines. To advocate the use of latrines without recognizing the wider implications of what going to the fields means for the women would be to chance rejection of the whole idea (ibid.: 1504). New health practices are seldom accepted if they challenge tenaciously-held beliefs and practices central to the client's culture, in this instance, a long-standing form of social interaction. The client's culture must be understood as it relates to the client's everyday world. Though Paul's ideas and recommendations were written over thirty years ago, their relevance still holds, for where culture is concerned, nurses must 'come to grips with a subject much wider than a few traditional habits relating to disease' (Parry 1984: 49) if they are to promote new health ideas that clients will accept and maintain.

NURSING, HEALTH AND CULTURE

The relevance of cultural factors to health care, and to nursing care, is well recognized by theoretically-oriented social scientists as well as by numerous health care practitioners (e.g. Leininger, 1967; Landy, 1977; Brownlee, 1978; Helman, 1985; Baxter, 1988), and is reflected in various statements in codes of conduct and ethics for nursing published by professional nursing bodies, for example:

- Inherent in nursing is respect for life, dignity and rights of man. It is unrestricted by considerations of nationality, race, creed, colour, age, sex, politics or social status. (ICN, 1973: 1)

- The nurse, in providing care, promotes an environment in which the values, customs and spiritual beliefs of the individual are respected. (ibid.)

- Each registered nurse, midwife and health visitor is accountable for his or her practice, and, in the exercise of professional accountability shall . . . take account of the customs, values and spiritual beliefs of patients/clients. (UKCC, 1984: 2)

- Individualized programs of nursing care are designed to accommodate the psychological, social, cultural and spiritual needs of clients, as well as their biological needs. (CNA 1985: 4)

Providing culturally appropriate nursing care can be very challenging, requiring much thought and caring concern, and a willingness to learn from those we nurse. Whatever the area of practice, nursing care should exude cultural sensitivity, understanding and respect. Not only must nurses be aware of the client's cultural 'point of view, his relation to life, to realise *his* vision of *his* world' (Malinowski, 1922: 25), but be willing to look at health needs and problems in new ways, planning nursing interventions that are culturally acceptable and meaningful to the client. Although planning and providing care that is congruent with the client's culture, and as the client sees this to be, may require extra time and effort, the nurse is not left 'empty-handed' (Cohen, 1982: 14); potential benefits for the nurse include: 'expanding cultural awareness, growth as an independent practitioner, fulfillment of professional responsibilities, and development of a comparative perspective' (ibid.: 10).

In many countries, nursing is shaped by the norms of the dominant culture, and there may be little leeway for the acceptance and inclusion of other approaches to life and living. While many nurses may find it difficult to change their ideas on how a patient should behave while in hospital, it can be all too easy to label patients as uncooperative (Macgregor, 1967) or for them to become 'unpopular' (Stockwell, 1972) because they act and react in ways that are culturally different from what is expected of them, perhaps sitting cross-legged on their bed or eating with their fingers rather than with cutlery, as might be the preferred practice of an Indian (East) or Pakistani patient (Henley, 1983: 85). It can be helpful, and indeed salutary, for nurses to look at some of their own cultural traditions and spend a moment wondering how they arose, and why they are maintained. What, for instance, do 'time-honoured' British traditions such as the wedding cake and the bride's bouquet symbolize (e.g. Charsley, 1985)? Examples not linked in any way to health, but vivid cultural traditions that are invariably taken for granted as being essential to all weddings. Many nursing practices, and indeed nurses' expectations of patients, are also perpetuated over time and seldom questioned, and many of them may seem strange or unacceptable to someone from another culture.

In most cultures there are several forms of health care to which an individual or a family may turn. People who wish to be helped or healed will turn to practitioners whose care is considered efficacious, accessible and relevant to their cultural view and needs. It is also not unusual for people to turn to more than one health care practitioner at the same time, or serially should the health problem persist. The Pakistani Muslim, for instance, whether living in Britain or the Subcontinent, may consult a *hakim* (a traditional herbal

Fig. 7   An Anglo/Scottish wedding

healer, who practises *Unani* medicine) as well as a doctor of the Western scientific tradition for the same concern (Aslam, Davis and Stockley, 1981; Rack, 1982: 188). A person in Taiwan may choose to visit a *tâng-ki* (a sacred healer) or perhaps a 'Chinese-style' or 'Western-style' doctor (Kleinman, 1980: e.g. 188–9). When ill, the Jamaican, whether living in Jamaica or Britain, may draw upon a 'triple insurance policy', a combination of at least three different measures: 'scientific medicine, herbal medicine and Christian prayer in the hope that the illness will be resolved' (Chevannes, 1989: 50). And, just as traditional healers are part of most cultures, so are folk practices and remedies. By tradition, the British feed a cold and starve a fever (Helman, 1978), and, in certain parts of England, the recently delivered mother is restricted from visiting within the local community until she has been 'churched', a religious rite of passage that still carries a sense of ritual purification for some (Staton, 1981).

It is also important for nurses to know what their patients consider to be the causation of ill-health and misfortune, and what they see as appropriate measures for dealing with such events. If the patient does not believe in germs as the precursors of ill-health or that carelessness can precede an accident, then it is unlikely that he/she will accept advice involving taking precautions of this type against such events. The rationale for 'why there are no accidents in Thika' (Wilkinson, 1986), for example, is part of the cultural logic of the Kikuyu of Kenya. For the Kikuyu patient who views a fractured leg, for instance, to be the result of someone wishing him harm, any suggestion that the injury might have been the result of consuming too much drink to allow him to balance on a roofing beam, which being wet made balancing all the more difficult, has little relevance. Misfortune does not just happen, 'someone must be responsible' (Wilkinson, 1986: 50). Appropriate nursing care in such instances involves promoting the reduction of anxiety. This includes ensuring that family members and friends are free to visit to reassure the patient that they wish him no harm.

Nurses also need to be alert to signs and symptoms attributed to one particular illness and its complications in one culture being differently construed in another culture. Western medical practitioners, for example, see dehydration as a serious complication of childhood diarrhoea. For the families in Vellore in south India, about whom Lozoff, Kamath, and Feldman (1975) write, diarrhoea (*behdi*) and dehydration (*dosham*) are conceptually different entities. While the former is considered a disturbance of function and amenable to Western medicine (which the writers refer to as 'international medicine'), the latter indicates a state of cultural pollution which requires ritual purification. The child with *dosham* will be saved only if he or she is purified, notions of purity and impurity being central themes of traditional Indian culture. A child with diarrhoea who then develops dehydration may not be brought back to the international medical practitioner, not because the family is uncaring, but because their concern leads them instead to seek ritual purification. Certain chants (*mantram*) need to be recited and, if necessary, a thread-tying ceremony performed. This highlights the importance, when applicable, of nurses and other health professionals working as partners in care with religious healers.

Although we know that numerous cultures exist world-wide, it is not always easy for us to step outside our own cultural view and look at the world from a different cultural perspective. Yet, if health is to be promoted to the client's satisfaction and individualized nursing care is to be offered, nurses must be able to emancipate themselves from their own cultural view and consider life as through a different cultural lens. Identifying what is pertinent information about a client's culture in relation to a particular nursing situation and finding ways to make nursing care culturally acceptable is nothing less than essential. While exploring the realms of another culture is a fascinating activity, and one can emerge from such an experience immensely knowledgeable about one culture, how does such knowledge become useful to nursing practice and to increasing clien‹ satisfaction?

In an article entitled 'Adapting health care to a cultural setting', Glittenberg (1974), a North American nurse, describes how Dr Behrhorst developed a hospital which blended Western medical traditions into the lifeways of the Cakchiquel Indians of Guatemala, descendants of the ancient Mayas, rather than constraining them to adapt their ways to fit in with the expectations of Western health professionals. Here is a glimpse into the life of this particular hospital:

> Family ties are very strong in this Mayan tribe, and family life is not disrupted by hospitalization of a member. Each 'bed' becomes a home for the family; familiar bedding, pots, and pans are brought along. Familiar foods are cooked on the open fire in the 'kitchen'. (Glittenberg, 1974: 2221)

While life in this Guatemalan hospital is a far cry from that in most major city hospitals in North America, or in the United Kingdom, the abiding principle, that of nurses and doctors providing culturally sensitive and meaningful care which allows people to feel a sense of dignity in regard to their cultural traditions, applies no less. And it should apply in whatever area of practice nurses work, be it midwifery, school nursing, coronary care or community nursing, though it may be much more difficult to achieve if the pace of the clinical area is fast, patients are from diverse ethnic groups and patient turnover is rapid.

In some instances, providing culturally relevant advice may be reasonably straightforward. A health visitor, for instance, might be in the position to advise a playgroup supervisor that culture-specific items are needed if Punjabi pre-schoolers are to create imaginary homes based on their personal lifestyle. Recommended items might include a saucepan for making Indian-style tea, *chapatti* board and rolling pin, greeting cards of religious festivals such as *Eid* and *Diwali*, and material for making saris, trousers and tunic outfits (*salwar-kamee*) and turbans for Asian dolls (Glass, 1975: 19). But it is much more complex, however, to provide culturally-sensitive care for clients with concerns that assume dimensions of a more intricate, personal and long-term nature, which might be the situation when advising and supporting a British Asian suffering from coronary heart disease or a native Canadian incest victim (see HEA, 1988; CCSD, 1988).

Racial and economic factors compound many health situations that ethnic minority people face, and a nurse from another culture needs to feel his/her way, looking at each client's needs from the client's perspective, providing the appropriate support and care, or else referring the client, if he or she so wishes, to someone who can. For many adolescent native Canadian Indians, life has involved facing difficult and recurrent social, economic and interracial situations, and much support may be needed if the adolescent is to achieve a lasting sense of self-esteem (Sinclair, 1987). In such situations, finding someone from the same ethnic community to act as a 'Big Brother' or 'Big Sister' may be one form of long-term support, both the Big Brother and the Big Sister organizations being concerned to provide a young person with support and guidance through a Big Brother–Little Brother or Big Sister–Little Sister relationship (see, Lichtenberg, 1956; Beiswinger, 1985). For the ethnic minority elder living in an inner-city area in Britain, there may be isolation, deprivation and poverty to cope with, in addition to cultural needs. Although it can be difficult for anyone who is old to live in a deprived inner-city area, it can be particularly difficult if one is 'old and black or ethnically different' (Age Concern, 1984: 19).

While all nurses in multicultural societies potentially care for people from diverse cultural backgrounds and need to be proficient in providing culturally relevant nursing care, there is also much merit in care being provided by nurses from the client's own ethnic group. With different cultures having their own styles of teaching and preferred ways of learning, a nurse from another culture may have difficulty, at least until well-versed in the ways of the particular culture, not only in using skilfully the 'teachable moment' (Nash, 1938), but in using a culture-specific style of teaching with an air of authenticity. For the Ojibway Indians of Canada, story-telling is one important means of teaching, and one that was used in a Native Diabetes Program in Toronto. In creating and recounting the Story of Nanabush and the Pale Stranger, the concern of diabetes and the need for its control among the Ojibway was placed within a new and different explanatory framework, offering a much more powerful and relevant message to the Ojibway diabetic by being presented in culturally meaningful terms (Hagey, 1984). The story tells of the legendary figure, Nanabush, who represents 'the teacher in Ojibway culture' and of 'his first encounter with the personified character of Diabetes' (Hagey, 1984: 265). As no one can lie to Nanabush, what 'Diabetes tells Nanabush is taken to be the truth about himself' (ibid.). At the various workshops that were held, everyone sat in a circle and explanations were given as to

> the way in which the circle represents the Native community in harmony with nature: birds make their nests in a circle, the earth turns in a circle, the Indian people dance in a circle, the most powerful forces of nature such as cyclones turn in a circle. Childhood, youth, adulthood and old age are the four seasons of life which form a circle. (ibid.: 266)

People attending were thus encouraged to look at the health and social problems that challenge the diabetic Ojibway through Ojibway approaches to life and learning.

Another example of how health promotion might be

delivered in a more culturally relevant way concerns a phone-in project in London, in which health professionals fluent in various ethnic minority languages offered guidance on health problems. As an approach to helping people, it was particularly well used by Asians, though less so by Afro-Caribbean people (Webb, 1981). It transpired that many of the concerns that people voiced had been inadequately dealt with, or not at all, by health professionals (e.g. general practitioners). The success of this project among the London Asian population was considered to be because it 'fitted in to a culturally accepted pattern' (Webb, 1981: 147). Those giving advice 'spoke the right language, they understood the cultural roots and they tried to talk about the whole patient and his family' (ibid.). Hence, it was similar in many ways to the care offered by *hakims*, traditional Asian healers who practise in Britain as well as in the Subcontinent. For the most part, the concerns that people voiced were not those identified by the medical profession nor those addressed by health educators, a finding that has relevance to health visitors in their search for health needs.

Using the same language and understanding the same symbolic meanings are obviously of enormous help when promoting client health, and are what happens when nurses visit clients from their own culture, though social class differences can militate against intra- as well as intercultural understanding and empathy. Nevertheless, bringing ideas from one culture to another can add an element of novelty, if the general approach is acceptable. A health carnival, for example, which spanned several days and was organized by a West Indian nurse, was held several years ago in an Inuit village, apparently with great success. The ways in which nurses can meld culture and care are innumerable, much depending on the client's needs and situation on the one hand, and the nurse's ingenuity and willingness to take time to understand another person's cultural ways on the other.

REFERENCES

Nursing

Benner P and Wrubel J (1989) *The Primacy of Caring. Stress and coping in health and illness.* Menlo Park, CA: Addison-Wesley.

Bhanumathi PP (1977) Nurses' conceptions of 'sick role' and 'good patient' behaviour. A cross-cultural comparison. *International Nursing Review* **24**(1): 20–4.

Colliere MF (1986) Invisible care and invisible women as health care-providers. *International Journal of Nursing Studies* **23**(2): 95–112.

Donaldson SK and Crowley DM (1978) The discipline of nursing. *Nursing Outlook* **26**(2): 113–20.

Johnson DE (1961) The significance of nursing care. *American Journal of Nursing* **61**(11): 63–6.

Kerslake MT (1988) Across cultures. *New Zealand Nursing Journal* **81**(1): 20–2.

Kubricht DW and Clark JA (1982) Foreign patients: A system for providing care. *Nursing Outlook* **30**(1): 55–7.

Leininger M (1981) The phenomenon of caring: Importance, research questions and theoretical considerations. In MM Leininger (ed.), *Caring. An essential human need.* Thorofare, NJ: Slack.

Lennon P (1974) A foreign patient suffering from acute renal failure. *Nursing Times* **70**(44): 1688–90.

Lipe HP (1980) The function of weeping in the adult. *Nursing Forum* **19**(1): 26–44.

Morse JM (1984) The cultural context of infant feeding in Fiji. *Ecology of Food and Nutrition* **14**: 287–96.

Nightingale F (1860) *Notes on Nursing. What it is, and what it is not.* London: Harrison.

Peplau HE (1952) *Interpersonal Relations in Nursing. A conceptual frame of reference for psychodynamic nursing.* New York: Putnam.

Rogers ME (1970) *An Introduction to the Theoretical Basis of Nursing.* Philadelphia: Davis.

Roy C and Roberts SL (1981) *Theory Construction in Nursing. An adaptation model.* Englewood Cliffs, NJ: Prentice Hall.

Tao-Kim-Hai AM (1965) Orientals are stoic. In JK Skipper and RC Leonard (eds), *Social Interaction and Patient Care.* Philadelphia: Lippincott.

Tatton-Brown W (1978) Owed to the Nightingale. *Nursing Times* **74**(31): 1273–8.

Taylor EP and Cooper DK (1972) Hospital care in the Indian Punjab. *Nursing Times* **68**(29): 912–14.

Watson J (1979) *Nursing. The philosophy and science of caring.* Boston, MA: Little, Brown.

Whitethread M (1981) Ostomists. A world of difference. *Journal of Community Nursing* **5**(2): 4–5, 10.

Health

Billington R (ed.) (1978) *Health has Many Faces*. London: Conference of British Missionary Societies.

Brent Community Health Council (1981) *Black People and the Health Service*. London: Brent Community Health Council.

Brubaker BH (1983) Health promotion: a linguistic analysis. *Advances in Nursing Science* **5**(3): 1–14.

Cardenas B and Lucarz J (1985) Canadian Indian health care. A model for service. In M Stewart, J Innes, S Searl and C Smillie (eds), *Community Health Nursing in Canada*. Toronto: Gage.

CETHV (Council for the Education and Training of Health Visitors) (1977) *An Investigation into the Principles of Health Visiting*. London: CETHV.

DHSS (Department of Health and Social Security) (1980) *Inequalities in Health*. Report of a research working group (The Black Report). Chairman: Sir D Black. London: DHSS.

Dunn HL (1959) What high-level wellness means. *Canadian Journal of Public Health* **50**(11): 447–57.

Fawcett J (1984) *Analysis and Evaluation of Conceptual Models of Nursing*. Philadelphia: Davis.

Health and Welfare Canada (1986) *Achieving Health for All. A framework for health promotion*. Ottawa: Health and Welfare Canada.

Health and Welfare Canada (1988) *Canada's Food Guide Handbook (Revised)*. Ottawa: Health and Welfare Canada.

Higgins C and Lewin L (1971) Down on the Bayou. *Nursing Forum* **10**(2): 122–31.

Hubley J (1979) *A Community Development Approach to Health Education in a Multiply-deprived Community in Scotland*. Paper presented to the 10th International Conference on Health Education in London. 4 September.

Jago JD (1975) 'Hal' – Old word, new task. Reflections on the words 'health' and 'medical'. *Social Science and Medicine* **9** (1): 1–6.

Keller MJ (1981) Toward a definition of health. *Advances in Nursing Science* **4**(1): 43–64.

Labonte R (1989) Community and professional empowerment. *The Canadian Nurse* **85**(3): 23–6, 28.

Mahler H (1981) The meaning of 'health for all by the year 2000'. *World Health Forum* **2**(1): 5–22.

Mares P (1982) *The Vietnamese in Britain. A handbook for health workers.* Cambridge: Health Education Council/National Extension College.

Paul BD (ed.) (1955) Introduction. Understanding the community. In *Health, Culture and Community. Case studies of public reactions to health programs.* New York: Russell Sage.

Payne L (1983) Health: a basic concept in nursing theory. *Journal of Advanced Nursing* **8**(5): 393–5.

Rootman I (1988) Inequities in health. Sources and solutions. *Health Promotion*, Winter: 2–8.

Seedhouse D (1986) *Health. The foundations for achievement.* Chichester: John Wiley.

Sigman PM (1979) Student's viewpoint: A challenge to the concept of adaptation as 'healthy'. *Advances in Nursing Science* **1**(4): 85–90.

Sissons J (1968) *Judge of the Far North. The memoirs of Jack Sissons.* Toronto: McClelland & Stewart.

Smith JA (1981) The idea of health: A philosophical inquiry. *Advances in Nursing Science* **3**(3): 43–50.

Social Insurance and Allied Services (1942) Report by Sir William Beveridge. Cmd 6404. London: HMSO.

WHO (World Health Organization) (1978) *Primary Health Care.* Report of the International Conference on Primary Health Care, Alma-Ata, USSR, 6–12 September. Geneva: World Health Organization.

Winstead-Fry P (1980) The scientific method and its impact on holistic health. *Advances in Nursing Science* **2**(4): 1–7.

Culture

Eliot TS (1948) *Notes towards the Definition of Culture.* London: Faber & Faber.

Frake CO (1977) Plying frames can be dangerous. Some reflections on methodology in cognitive anthropology. *The Quarterly Newsletter of the Institute for Comparative Human Development* **1**(3): 1–7.

Helman C (1985) *Culture, Health and Illness.* Bristol: Wright.

Leach E (1976) *Culture and Communication.* Cambridge University Press.

Leach E (1982) *Social Anthropology.* London: Fontana.

Leininger M (ed.) (1978) *Transcultural Nursing. Concepts, theories, and practices.* New York: John Wiley.
Lewis IM (1976) *Social Anthropology in Perspective.* Harmondsworth: Penguin Books.
Mead M (1953) *Cultural Patterns and Technical Change.* Paris: World Federation for Mental Health, UNESCO.
Parry EH (1984) The influence of culture. *World Health Forum* **5**(1): 49–52.
Paul BD (1958) The role of beliefs and customs in sanitation programs. *American Journal of Public Health* **48**(11): 1502–6.
Spradley JP (1979) *The Ethnographic Interview.* New York: Holt, Rinehart & Winston.
Temple C and Henderson V (1978) Communication, human relations, learning, health goals and guidance. In V Henderson and G Nite (eds), *Principles and Practice of Nursing*, 6th edition. New York: Macmillan.
Tylor EB (1871) *Primitive Culture. Researches into the development of mythology, philosophy, religion, art, and custom, 1.* London: John Murray.

Nursing, Health and Culture

Age Concern (1984) *Housing for Ethnic Elders.* Report of a working party set up by Age Concern England and Help the Aged Housing Trust to examine housing and related problems among elders in ethnic minorities. Chairman: J Bartlett. Mitcham: Age Concern/Help the Aged Housing Trust.
Aslam M, Davis S and Stockley I (1981) In the best of traditions? *Nursing Mirror* **153**(4): 34–6.
Baxter C (1988) Culture shock. *Nursing Times* **84**(2): 36–8.
Beiswinger GL (1985) *One to One. The story of the Big Brothers/Big Sisters movement in America.* Philadelphia: Big Brothers/Big Sisters of America.
Brownlee AT (1978) *Community, Culture, and Care. A cross-cultural guide for health workers.* St Louis: CV Mosby.
CCSD (Canadian Council on Social Development) (1988) Telephone network links Inuit incest victims. *Vis-à-vis* **5**(4): 6.
Charsley S (1985) *Marriage Rites in One's Own Society. The problem of meaning.* Paper given at the conference of 'Anthropology at Home' held by the Association of Social Anthropologists at the University of Keele. 26 March.
Chevannes M (1989) Childrearing among Jamaican families in Britain. *Health Visitor* **62**(2): 48–51.

CNA (Canadian Nurses Association) (1985) *Code of Ethics for Nursing*. Ottawa: CNA.

Cohen FS (1982) Transcultural nursing. Benefits for the nurse. *Nursing Leadership* 5(1) 10–14.

Glass V (1975) Multiculture Wendy House. *Teacher's World*, No. 3415: 19.

Glittenberg J (1974) Adapting health care to a cultural setting. *American Journal of Nursing* 74(12): 2218–21.

Hagey R (1984) The phenomenon, the explanations and the responses: Metaphors surrounding diabetes in urban Canadian Indians. *Social Science and Medicine* 18(3): 265–72.

HEA (Health Education Authority) (1988) *Heart-health and Asians in Britain*. Report of a workshop organized by the Health Education Authority and Coronary Prevention Group. London: Health Education Authority.

Helman CG (1978) 'Feed a cold, starve a fever'. Folk models of infection in an English suburban community, and their relation to medical treatment. *Culture, Medicine and Psychiatry* 2: 107–37.

Helman C (1985) *Culture, Health and Illness*. Bristol: Wright.

Henley A (1983) Monocultural health services in a multicultural society. In J Clark and J Henderson (eds), *Community Health*. Edinburgh: Churchill Livingstone.

ICN (International Council of Nurses) (1973) *Code for Nurses. Ethical concepts applied to nursing*. Geneva: ICN.

Kleinman A (1980) *Patients and Healers in the Context of Culture*. Berkeley, CA: University of California Press.

Landy D (ed.) (1977) *Culture, Disease, and Healing. Studies in medical anthropology*. New York: Macmillan.

Leininger M (1967) The culture concept and its relevance to nursing. *Journal of Nursing Education* 6(2): 27–37.

Lichtenberg B (1956) On the selection and preparation of the Big Brother volunteer. *Social Casework* 37(8): 396–400.

Lozoff B, Kamath KR and Feldman RA (1975) Infection and disease in South Indian families. Beliefs about childhood diarrhoea. *Human Organization* 34(4): 353–8.

Macgregor FC (1967) Uncooperative patients. Some cultural interpretations. *American Journal of Nursing* 67(1): 88–91.

Malinowski B (1922) *Argonauts of the Western Pacific*. London: Routledge & Kegan Paul.

Nash JB (1938) *Teachable moments. A new approach to health*. New York: AS Barnes.

Rack P (1982) *Race, Culture, and Mental Disorder*. London: Tavistock.

Sinclair L (1987) Native adolescents in crisis. *The Canadian Nurse* **83**(8): 28–9.

Staton M (1981) Churching – Past and present. *Contact* [Journal of Pastoral Studies], No. 72: 10–17.

Stockwell F (1972) *The Unpopular Patient*. London: Royal College of Nursing.

UKCC (United Kingdom Central Council for Nursing, Midwifery and Health Visiting) (1984) *Code of Professional Conduct for the Nurse, Midwife and Health Visitor*, 2nd edn. London: UKCC.

Webb P (1981) Health problems of London's Asian and Afro-Caribbeans. *Health Visitor* **54**(4): 141, 144–5, 147.

Wilkinson S (1986) Why there are no accidents in Thika. *Nursing Times* **82**(18): 49–51.

CHAPTER 3

The Development of Transcultural Nursing

Two themes dominated the previous two chapters: the first, that many countries the world over are multicultural societies, and the second, that culture is an important factor in the provision of relevant, client-centred nursing care. In this chapter, we shall look at the development of transcultural nursing both in North America and in the United Kingdom. Whether nurses care for clients from only one or two differing cultural groups or from a wide diversity of cultural heritages, it is important that nurses be skilled in providing culturally appropriate care. Where nurse and client are from the same cultural group, nursing care is provided on an *intra*cultural basis. Where nurse and client are from different cultures, then nursing assumes *inter*cultural dimensions and nurses need to be proficient in nursing transculturally. This, however, involves more than being aware of specific cultural customs, it involves nurses being knowledgeable about how such customs interrelate and the value orientations that shape the cultural whole. It also involves nurses recognizing themselves as cultural beings who, like their clients, think, feel, act and react in culture-specific ways.

As a field of nursing, it is perhaps not surprising that 'transcultural nursing' should have its roots in the United States, a country comprising people from such a wide diversity of cultural heritages. In this chapter, an overview of the genesis of transcultural nursing in the United States and its development in North America is followed by a discussion on the cultural dimension of nursing in the United Kingdom. As the term 'transcultural nursing' has not been in regular use for as long in British nursing as it has in North American nursing, the term 'multicultural' will be used in this chapter in relation to intercultural nursing in the United Kingdom.

While the focus of this chapter is on the development of transcultural/multicultural nursing in only three of the numerous countries that offer recognized nurse education programmes (e.g. International Nursing Foundation of Japan, 1977), multicultural awareness in nursing is developing in other countries (e.g. Australia) and in all probability will become an important area of nursing concern in many more countries in the years ahead. Being able to offer culturally-sensitive and relevant care is also important to the nurse who works in intercultural situations for organizations such as Voluntary Service Overseas (VSO), Canadian University Service Overseas (CUSO) and Save the Children Fund. One might argue that there is no need to view 'transcultural nursing' as a specialist area of nursing in that cultural factors should always be among those considered in all instances of nursing practice. Since this has not always been the case in the past, and even yet cultural factors are not necessarily considered routinely, specific emphasis on multi-/transcultural nursing would seem justified.

UNITED STATES OF AMERICA AND CANADA

As long ago as the late 1940s, it was recognized that nurses caring for patients and clients from 'diverse origins and life situations' (Brown, 1964: 14) needed 'considerable social science knowledge', such as sociology, social psychology and anthropology, 'at their disposal, as well as experience in using that knowledge' (Brown, 1964: 11, 14; also Macgregor, 1960). Esther Lucile Brown (1948), whose report *Nursing for the Future* spearheaded mid-century reform in nurse educa-

Fig. 8   VSO work being carried out in Gambia

tion in the United States (Dougherty and Tripp-Reimer, 1985: 221), was herself an anthropologist. A number of nurses who realized the need to understand cultural differences while serving with the military during the Second World War were also among those who were influential in promoting cultural content in nursing curricula. In public health nursing, however, the relevance of the client's culture to nursing care has been recognized since the early 1900s. Indeed, Lillian Wald, renowned for developing a visiting nursing service in the early days of the twentieth century in the slums of East Side, New York, describes in some detail the religious and cultural variations of her clientele in her classic text, *The House on Henry Street* (Wald, 1915; also Davis and Haasis, 1920).

Although many nurses have been involved in the development of transcultural nursing in North America, Madeleine Leininger is acknowledged as the pioneer, nurturing the growth and development of transcultural nursing from the late 1960s onwards. Leininger defines transcultural nursing as focusing on

> the comparative study and analysis of different cultures and subcultures with respect to nursing and health-illness caring practices, beliefs, and values with the goal of generating scientific and humanistic knowledge and of using this knowledge to provide culture-specific and culture-universal nursing care practices. (Leininger, 1978: 493)

A more easily remembered explanatory quotation describes transcultural nursing as understanding and helping 'cultural groups with their nursing and health care needs with full thought to culture-specific values, beliefs, and practices' (ibid.: 8). In her book, *Transcultural Nursing: Concepts, theories, and practices*, Leininger (1978) explains how, as a psychiatric clinical nurse specialist at a guidance home for disturbed children in the mid-1950s, she became increasingly dissatisfied with the then current psychoanalytical theories used to explain and predict child and adult behaviour as well as to determine nursing interventions. Caring for children from a variety of cultural backgrounds, such as Appalachian and Afro-American, she noticed that the children exhibited great behavioural differences in activities such as playing, eating and sleeping. During her subsequent studies in anthropology, she realized that anthropological knowledge and insights could help to provide nurses with a 'broad, comparative background' with which to 'understand human behavior and cultural groups' (ibid.: 22).

Since then, an increasing number of nurses in North America have studied anthropology, and the contribution that anthropological knowledge and insights can provide to the provision of culturally-sensitive nursing care continues to be well recognized (see e.g. Chrisman, 1982). Dougherty and Tripp-Reimer (1985: 221–2) provide a brief overview of the development of cultural awareness in nursing in an article addressing the interface of nursing and anthropology. They note a number of significant landmarks including the formation of the Council on Nursing and Anthropology in 1968 and the decision in 1977, by the National League for Nursing, to mandate the inclusion of cultural content in nursing curricula.

Fig. 9 Dr. Leininger 'in the field' – visiting the Gadsup women of New
Guinea as they prepare the family meal

Many nurses in the United States and in Canada have
contributed, and continue to contribute, to a growing
literature relating to the cultural dimension of nursing.
Several texts, and chapters in texts, have been published
(e.g. Branch and Paxton, 1976; Aamodt, 1978; Orque, Bloch
and Monrroy, 1983; Tripp-Reimer, 1984a; and Glasgow and
Adaskin, 1990) offering insights and guidelines for nurses
practising in multicultural situations, particularly for
nurses caring for ethnic minority groups. Tripp-Reimer
(1984a), for example, brings together a range of ideas and
guidelines to assist nurses in making culturally appropriate
assessments. She stratifies culture into three layers. In
descending order, these layers are: customs, beliefs and
values. Values, the most difficult to assess as least apparent,
are assigned to the foundational, bottom tier. In addition to
these publications, many ideas, experiences and research
findings pertaining to the cultural dimension of nursing
have been presented in journal articles (e.g. Aichlmayr,

1969; Hodgson, 1980; Satz, 1982). Research studies include those by Bonaparte (1979) and Jaffe Ruiz (1981) who consider nurses' attitudes to 'culturally different' patients, Jaffe Ruiz specifically looking at the attitudes of nursing faculty. Other studies look at racial concerns. Morgan (1983), for instance, looks at white nursing students' attitudes towards black American patients and addresses the sensitive, multi-dimensional and important question of racial prejudice.

Ethnic/cultural diversity exists within all racial groups, and studies such as Tripp-Reimer (1983) on urban Greek immigrants, Aamodt (1981) on the neighbouring practices of Norwegian-American women and Ragucci (1971; 1972) on Italian-Americans are important in that they alert nurses to the diversity that exists among white people. The first study highlights the need to consider the maintenance of traditional health care practices from an intergenerational perspective. Even though an individual maintains 'high ethnic affiliation' (Tripp-Reimer, 1983: 101), traditional health behaviours are not necessarily retained. Ragucci (1972), who considers persistence and change of traditional health beliefs and associated practices, adds an extra emphasis – intra- as well as intergenerational differences.

Several models developed by nurses in North America are now available for use in intercultural nursing situations. Leininger offers two, one being a 'conceptual and theory-generating model' for the study of transcultural and ethno-caring constructs (e.g. Leininger, 1981: 13). Comfort, empathy, nurturance and succorance are among the major ethno-caring and nursing care constructs listed, the term 'ethno-caring' referring to the typical folk classification or taxonomy of caring used in a given culture (see Ragucci, 1972: 486). The other model, Leininger's (1988: 157) 'Sunrise' model, relates to her nursing theory of cultural care diversity and universality, and may be used for 'culturologi-cal interviews, assessments, and therapy goals' (Leininger, 1984a: 116). This model (see also Chapter Four, page 119) emphasizes the use of three, culture-related nursing care decisions and actions: cultural care preservation, cultural care accommodation and cultural care repatterning, which may be used to 'fit the clients' cultural lifeways, norms, and

values in relevant, understandable, and meaningful ways',
helping thereby to reduce 'cultural stress and conflicts
between caregivers and clients' (Leininger, 1985: 210; also
1984a: 112–13). All three nursing care decisions and actions
pertain, each in its own way, to the client's cultural values,
beliefs and practices. As defined by Leininger (1988: 156):

> *Cultural care preservation* . . . refers to those assistive, suppor-
> tive, or enabling professional actions and decisions that help
> clients of a particular culture to preserve or maintain a state of
> health or to recover from illness and to face death.
> *Cultural care accommodation* . . . refers to those assistive, sup-
> porting, or enabling professional actions and decisions that
> help clients of a particular culture to adapt to or negotiate for a
> beneficial or satisfying health status or to face death.
> *Cultural care repatterning* . . . refers to those assistive, suppor-
> tive, or enabling professional actions or decisions that help
> clients change their lifeways for new or different patterns that
> are culturally meaningful and satisfying or that support benefi-
> cial and healthy life patterns.

Orque (1983) provides yet another model, the central part of
which she presented in 1981 in a similar format but specifically for use in maternity nursing. Orque's systems-based
model, which may be applied to patient or nurse, links basic
human needs with ethnic/cultural factors, which, in turn,
are seen as interrelating with sociological, biological and
psychological factors. Both Leininger's 'Sunrise' model and
Orque's (1983) model will be discussed further in the next
chapter (see Cultural assessment guides).

Two other models, both Canadian in origin, focus on the
care of immigrant clients. In one (Carpio, 1981) the focus is
on the adolescent immigrant who must cope with stresses
related to migration in addition to those linked to the
transition into adulthood. In this model, the pull of the
adolescent's culture of origin (the 'old' culture) is placed in
opposition to the pull of the 'new' host culture, the model
suggesting the presence of a dominant host culture. The
adolescent's family is part of the 'old' culture, with his/her
peers viewed as part of the 'new' culture. The notion of a host
culture is also reflected in Yoshida and Davies' (1985)
presentation, in a nursing text, of findings from a study of

'recent immigrant' families (Portuguese, Caribbean and East Indian) and 'Canadian' families in urban Toronto.

The other model (Davies and Yoshida, 1981), is concerned specifically with the assessment and care of the new immigrant, and focuses on three major areas: the client's 'country of origin', 'the receiving country' and the client's 'individuality'. The first-named area for consideration includes ecological factors such as climate and geography, as well as factors relating to social structure, such as education, politics, kinship, religion, economy and health care. The second-named area, that of the receiving country, is concerned with its similarities to and differences from the country of origin, and also the importance of other people living in the receiving country who are from the immigrant's country of origin. The third-named area includes the individual's 'reasons for emigration', 'adaptability to change' and 'acculturation'.

As Davies and Yoshida's model covers a wide gamut of concerns, including social and financial, it is likely that a cultural assessment based on this model would be best extended over several interview sessions, possibly two or three, as recommended by Leininger (1984a: 120) in regard to the culturological assessment format that she suggests. Recognizing that the patient is 'the primary source of information for the assessment', Davies and Yoshida (1981: 22) acknowledge the need to draw upon secondary sources to complete the assessment should, for instance, there be language barriers or a client be unable or unwilling 'to talk to the nurse or to understand what the nurse represents' (Davies and Yoshida, 1981: 22). Secondary sources include the literature, family members, immigrants from the same area of origin, and resource persons who work with people of the same nationality as that of the client (Davies and Yoshida, 1981). Although the article in which this model is presented lacks illustration of its use in everyday nursing practice, it is intended that findings from this immigrant-specific cultural assessment should be incorporated into the nurse's overall client assessment.

The relevance of cultural factors to nursing care has also been recognized by leading North American nurse theorists such as Neuman, King and Orem. Neuman (1985; also Sohier, 1989), whose systems model focuses on the concept of stress and possible stress reactions to stressors, includes 'sociocultural' as one of the variables (or 'parts') of the human being which are enclosed in her model by 'protective lines of defence and resistance' (Neuman, 1985: 21). In another model of nursing, one which is based on the notion of self-care, Orem (1985: 108) not only observes that: 'the activities of self-care are learned according to the beliefs, habits, and practices that characterize the cultural way of life of the group to which the individual belongs', but recognizes 'sociocultural orientation' to be one of several factors that set limits on the methods that nurses can select and use 'in meeting the self-care requisites of individuals' (ibid.: 163). King (1981: 3–4), for whom the goal of nursing is 'to help individuals maintain their health so they can function in their roles', sees health as relating to 'the way individuals deal with the stresses of growth and development while functioning within the cultural pattern in which they were born and to which they attempt to conform' (ibid.: 4).

Although the need for the inclusion of cultural concepts in nursing curricula is well accepted in Canada and the United States of America, at least in principle (e.g. Mattson, 1987), MacDonald (1987: 31) points out in an article in *The Canadian Nurse* that:

> In spite of all the discussions and literature on cross-cultural or transcultural nursing in recent years, the fact is that cross-cultural preparation for nurses today is given less emphasis in nursing education programs than other subjects . . . . Culture is often presented to nursing students almost as an afterthought.

Byerly (1977: 76–7) discusses the relevance in a school of nursing's philosophy and curriculum objectives of an explicit statement regarding the inclusion of cultural aspects of health care. Once a commitment to incorporate cultural dimensions into the nursing curriculum is made, she then sees the school assuming 'a parallel commitment to assure adequate preparation of those faculty who will teach the content' (ibid.: 77). In another article about cultural diversity in nursing curricula, Koshi (1976) places emphasis on the need to avoid categorizing people into groups, then labelling and typing them, when discussing cultural diversity. He observes that individualizing nursing care involves taking a number of variables such as social class, social status, skin colour and ethnicity into consideration, variables which he sees as affecting both the practitioner's and the patient's 'perceptions and responses' (Koshi, 1976: 15).

Nurse educators, such as Garner and Merrill (1976) and Fulton (1985), write about strategies they have used to bring about change with the intent to introduce increased cultural content in nursing curricula, while other nurse educators describe differing ways that cultural content may be incorporated into nursing curricula. Spector (1979: 301–6), for example, presents the outline of a nursing course entitled: *Cultural Diversity in Health and Illness*, the goal of which is 'to broaden the student's perception and understanding of health and illness and the variety of meanings it has to the members of ethnic groups of color' (ibid.: 302). A model for the inclusion of cultural diversity in nursing curricula is offered by Murillo-Rohde (1978: 458), the intent being that nurses will provide safe care for ethnic minorities. Two other nurses (Baker and Mayer, 1982) describe a student project they devised which included presentations on four different cultural groups, including White Anglo-Saxon Protestants (or WASP). By and large, the various approaches put forward for including cultural content in nursing curricula reflect three main approaches: threaded throughout the entire programme, within either a specific unit or several identified courses in the programme, or a combination of these approaches (e.g. Byerly, 1977; also Burrows, 1983: 483–4).

In the journal *Practicing Anthropology*, Lipson (1988: 5) describes ideas used and developed within an international and cross-cultural (ICC) nursing programme at the University of California at San Francisco:

> Because of the multiple goals of the ICC program, teaching requires a multi-pronged approach. The cultural perspective includes cognitive learning (knowledge, comprehension, analysis, synthesis), affective learning (experiential learning, work-

ing with feelings, attitudes and values), and skills (practice). The combination of clinical and personal experience, course work and reading with practice in multicultural health care situations works best.

In this programme, experiential learning includes each ICC student being paired with a new international student. The students are then required to meet for two hours each week in an activity of their choice (e.g. going out for a meal, sightseeing or learning word processing). As well as helping the new international student to adjust to the United States and to graduate nursing education, this part of the programme has provided the ICC student with 'a structured opportunity to quickly develop friendships and networking possibilities with peers from other countries' (Lipson, 1988: 5).

The focus of transcultural nursing in the North American continent continues to be directed towards the need for nurses, whether they work in hospital settings, such as intensive care units (Germain, 1982) or oncology departments (Clausen, 1978), or in the community (e.g. Aamodt, 1981), to provide culturally-sensitive and appropriate care. Boyle and Andrews' (1989) text, *Transcultural Concepts in Nursing Care*, addresses a wide range of issues and concerns, including those relating to pain (Ludwig-Beymer, 1989) and organ transplants (Kapsa, 1989), that have relevance to a variety of nursing practice settings. The value of a programme to help hospital nurses and other staff members become more adept in caring for clients from diverse cultural backgrounds has been recognized by the Montreal Children's Hospital. Located in the heart of multi-ethnic Montreal, this hospital has developed an active multiculturalism programme to promote interest and to assist nursing and non-nursing staff in the provision of culturally-sensitive and appropriate patient care (e.g. Laughlin, 1989).

Developments in transcultural nursing in North America include the emergence of university-based masters and doctoral programmes with a clear transcultural nursing focus (e.g. at Wayne State University, Detroit; University of Miami, Florida) and the growth of the Transcultural Nursing Society which holds annual conferences, most of which

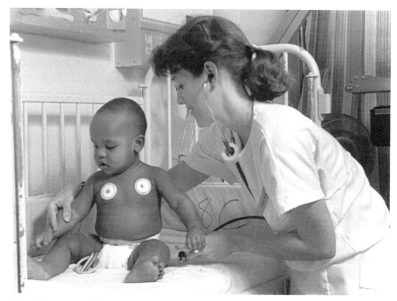

Fig. 10   An Italian nurse caring for a Somalian baby at Montreal
Children's Hospital

have been held in Canada and the United States of America
(Brink, 1984: 131–2; Leininger, 1984b: 72). These conferences
provide nurses interested in transcultural nursing with
additional opportunities to share ideas and research findings with each other. They have focused on a variety of
topics including specific patient and client groups, the
alignment of theoretical thinking with practice, and ethical
issues such as cultural imposition. There is now increased
recognition in North America that research priorities need
to be directed not only towards theoretical development in
transcultural nursing but also towards the application of
research findings to clinical nursing practice (see Tripp-
Reimer, 1984b: 254–5).

For the most part, transcultural nursing in Canada and
the United States has developed in the context of North
American nursing. Even so, there has been a certain
recognition of its relevance to the preparation of nurses for

working internationally. Leininger, for example, presented her ideas on transcultural nursing in 1979 at an international nursing conference sponsored by Project Hope, an organization that helps provide health care to people in underprivileged countries. Lipson (1988) also advocates the importance of cultural awareness, as it relates to both self and others, in relation to the development of international nursing expertise.

Transcultural nursing has clearly made many developmental strides since its genesis in the late 1960s. However, in discussing the relevance of transcultural nursing to international nursing, DeSantis (1988) suggests that more emphasis should be directed towards the area of policy decision-making as it applies to the international health care arena. While recognizing the importance of the cultural variable in the implementation and evaluation stages of health care programmes, policy-makers usually ignore the cultural variable during planning stages. DeSantis advises nurses to help make policy-makers constantly aware of cultural factors by helping them to draw out cultural variables when the social impact of a health care programme is being assessed. Questions asked must address

> the social costs of planned programmes, the target group's perceptions of its needs, the community's ability to participate, the ethnomedical knowledge of health care professionals, and the ability and willingness of health care professionals and others to carry through programmes and work with traditional healers and village-level workers. (DeSantis, 1988: 111)

If the nurse is to influence public health policy-makers as to the relevance of transcultural research findings, DeSantis (ibid.: 112) recommends that the nurse uses quantitative as well as qualitative research methods so that findings can be more readily generalized to a whole population. DeSantis (1988: 112) also recommends that the nurse places increased reliance on computer analysis, keeps social service jargon to a minimum and is well-informed about 'the methods, theories, concepts and critical issues guiding the formulations of policies and programmes'. Indeed, if culturally appropriate nursing care is to be achieved and adequately funded, nurses must be influential at the macro- as well as at the micro-level, that is, at national level as well as at the client–nurse interface.

United Kingdom – Multicultural Nursing

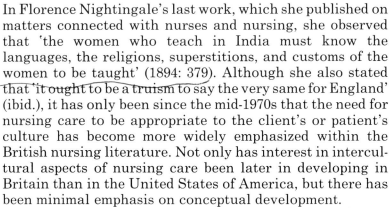

In Florence Nightingale's last work, which she published on matters connected with nurses and nursing, she observed that 'the women who teach in India must know the languages, the religions, superstitions, and customs of the women to be taught' (1894: 379). Although she also stated that 'it ought to be a truism to say the very same for England' (ibid.), it has only been since the mid-1970s that the need for nursing care to be appropriate to the client's or patient's culture has become more widely emphasized within the British nursing literature. Not only has interest in intercultural aspects of nursing care been later in developing in Britain than in the United States of America, but there has been minimal emphasis on conceptual development.

More articles with a clearer multicultural focus, and more clearly indexed as such in the nursing bibliography, began to emerge during the early 1970s, thus subsequent to the increase in immigration that occurred during the 1950s and 1960s. The needs of the immigrant, which may be wide-ranging and impinge on health in its broadest sense, provided Alexander (1974) with the theme for her article, 'Help for immigrant families', in which she points out the importance of cultural insight not only for nurses, but for all health workers:

> A knowledge of different patterns of culture is an asset to any worker concerned with health, since it increases understanding of the needs of people from different backgrounds and enables the worker to look for ways of meeting these needs which are effective because they are culturally acceptable. (Alexander, 1974: 632)

Although immigrants and refugees are unlikely to expect life in Britain to replicate life in their native land, coping with the reality of cultural differences and adjusting to li···· · in a new country may nevertheless be overwhelming me (ibid.: 634).

:e the mid-1970s, but particularly during the 1980s, the

number of articles addressing the cultural dimension to nursing care increased substantially. They have focused on a wide variety of concerns, including the lack of adequate financial resources and educational preparation for nurses to provide multiculturally and multiracially appropriate care (e.g. Karseras, 1988), and on specific fields of nursing practice, such as occupational nursing (e.g. Griffin, 1972) and health visiting (e.g. Wilson, 1988). The cultural ways and health concerns of Vietnamese refugees (e.g. Lam, 1980; Pearson, 1982), problems experienced by members of ethnic groups predisposed to sickle cell anaemia and thalassaemia (e.g. Anionwu and Beattie, 1981; May and Choiseul, 1988), the needs of South Asian women (e.g. Bunting, 1984; Turrell, 1985) and of ethnic minority elderly (e.g. Moore, 1984) are among the many topics relating to multicultural nursing which have received attention in recent years in the nursing press.

Although several texts have been written regarding the provision of culturally relevant health care in Britain (e.g. Lobo, 1978; Henley, 1979; Mares, 1982; Helman, 1985; Mares, Henley and Baxter, 1985; Fuller and Toon, 1988; Qureshi, 1989), there have been few texts which, specifically and in their entirety, address cultural aspects of *nursing* care in the United Kingdom. *The Neglected Ethic* (Sampson, 1982) and *British Asians: Health in the Community* (Karseras and Hopkins, 1987) are two British texts written by nurses and intended primarily for a nursing readership. In general, standard nursing texts that have addressed cultural and racial dimensions to nursing care have done so as the topic of either a specific chapter (e.g. Clark and Henderson, 1983) or a part of a chapter (e.g. Illing and Donovan, 1981) rather than being threaded throughout the entire text. For the most part, nurses must turn to journals for information on the delivery of multicultural nursing care, especially if they wish to read about ideas and experiences written by nurses for nurses. Unfortunately, some articles are not easily recognized as having multicultural content, that is, the title of the publication fails to indicate the intercultural nature of the care or concern described therein. One such publication is Crow's (1977) portrayal of cultural sensitivity in hospital nursing practice in which the nursing process is used as a basis for the care given to a Polish patient recovering from a fractured femur.

In the hospital setting, nurses are concerned with anticipating and responding to a wide range of patient needs, including those relating to acute or chronic pain, hygiene, appropriate and appetizing meals, and coping with death and dying, as well as the patient's need for meaningful communication with nurses and other health workers. As attitudes towards pain and suffering are to some extent a socially learned response, nurses working in intercultural situations must be alert to the possibility of marked cultural differences between what they and their patients consider acceptable external behaviour (Davitz and Davitz, 1985), lest unrecognized differences lead to misjudgements in the nurse's assessment of the patient's suffering. For patients whose fluency in English is minimal, access to adequate interpreting services is vital if they are to communicate their concerns and be active participants in all stages of the nursing process. Although cultural factors are very relevant to hospital nursing practice, more emphasis has been given in the British nursing literature to how cultural sensitivity enhances community nursing practice rather than instances of hospital or hospice nursing care.

In recent years, there has been a number of articles alerting nurses to the presence of racism both in nursing and in the British health service as a whole (e.g. Ellis, 1978; Pearson, 1986a and b; Carlisle, 1990). Publications have focused on the presence of racial prejudice and discrimination in the provision of nursing care and the employment of nursing personnel (e.g. Ayekoto, 1972; HEC, 1984; Mares, Henley and Baxter, 1985). Whether patient or nurse, to belong to a racial and to a cultural minority may require coping with the brunt of double prejudice. This increased recognition in recent years of the relevance of both racial and cultural factors to nursing care is possibly a reflection not only of changes within the nursing profession, but within the entire country. Indeed, to view the development of multicultural/multiracial awareness within the British nursing profession as separate from developments within the health and social services as a whole is to divorce nursing from the reality of its wider setting, for changes in one area invariably influence other areas.

National policies and directives that openly and affirmatively promote cultural sensitivity in nursing practice have been slow to emerge. Indeed, as reflected in the literature, concern for a multiculturally and multiracially sensitive health service generally has been more ardently vocalized, at least until recently, by non-nursing health and social service professionals than by the nursing profession. Numerous social scientists (e.g. Kitzinger, 1977; Ballard, 1979; Homans, 1982), for instance, as well as members of the medical profession (e.g. Dwivedi, 1980; Dunnigan [Dunnigan et al., 1981]; Littlewood and Lipsedge, 1982; Rack, 1982; Qureshi, 1985), other health and social service professionals, such as social workers (e.g. Coombe, 1976), dietitians (e.g. Attariwala, 1977) and health educators (e.g. Abbas, 1981), and various national and local organizations and institutions such as the Commission for Racial Equality (e.g. CRE, 1976) have led the way, with multicultural nursing practice developing more within multidisciplinary parameters than along nursing-specific tracks.

These numerous non-nursing professionals have provided much useful information which British nurses might draw upon to assist them in providing culturally astute and racially sensitive care in both institutional and community settings. Alix Henley (1979), for instance, a teacher of English as a second language, has written *Asian Patients in Hospital and at Home*, as well as articles in nursing journals, all of which have helped to alert nurses to the cultural norms of South Asian families and individuals. By and large, nursing in the United Kingdom has looked to others for knowledge and ideas relating to multicultural care and concerns. This is not to say that nurses have not contributed to the published literature on cultural concerns, for they clearly have. Their contributions, however, have tended to be pragmatic and sporadic rather than 'trail-blazing' and with clearly spelt-out directions. Until very recently, British nursing has generally lacked the energetic leadership in transcultural nursing that Leininger and other nurses and nurse-anthropologists have provided for North American nursing.

The non-nursing literature available to help guide nurses in their thinking and practice as this applies to the United Kingdom has covered many topics. Two articles (Davie, 1979; Bhaduri, 1979) describe care given by social workers to ethnic minority clients from the Indian Subcontinent. Both authors are concerned that their care should be sensitive and appropriate to the client's culture. Each article includes ideas which might easily be modified to the needs and ambit of nursing practice. In the first, which concerns a Punjabi Sikh family, Davie (1979) describes how using a task-centred casework approach helped the father of an educationally sub-normal teenage daughter with coeliac disease become more of a participant and an 'equal' (ibid.: 38) in the planning and provision of her care. In the second article, published in a nursing journal, Bhaduri (1979) describes cultural factors surrounding the terminal illness of a Bangladeshi boy and of her own reactions to the interpersonal tensions that emerged. Aware that mourning in the Subcontinent usually lasts for one month, during which time 'relatives, friends and neighbours come to see the bereaved and talk of the deceased person as they knew him', she aimed in her talks with the parents to highlight their recently deceased child 'in various perspectives, as a son, grandson, brother, school-child, cousin and nephew' (ibid. 638–9).

Psychiatrists are also among those who have taken an especially active interest in multi-/transcultural health care in the United Kingdom. Philip Rack, for instance, has been instrumental in developing a transcultural psychiatric unit in Bradford (see Knight, 1978: 14). His various publications provide guidance and ideas for a variety of health workers, including nurses. Dwivedi (1980), a family psychiatrist based in Tower Hamlets, London, has written about the use of 'Indian notions in counselling situations'. Illustrated throughout with Hindu and Buddhist parables, notions and mythological stories, this article highlights how different approaches to reducing emotional stress can be employed by those conversant with their client's religion and culture. Articles such as this act as reminders to British nurses and others professionally socialized into the Western medical belief system that cursorily to discredit non-Westernized health systems is to undermine approaches, treatments and therapies for care and cure that have been known for centuries to be efficacious and which are considered by many to be culturally satisfying.

Many papers and reports published by national and local, non-nursing organizations and institutions have also focused on the health and social needs of ethnic minority groups. Topics covered range from residential care for black children (CRE, 1977), services (including nursery nursing) for under fives from ethnic minority communities (DHSS, 1984), the provision of interpreter services and suitable diets for the hospitalized Asian patient (e.g. University of Manchester, 1981), to the life circumstances and health needs of specific ethnic minority groups such as the Chinese community in Lothian, Scotland (LCRC, 1983). This latter report provides insight into how the unsocial hours that many male Chinese restaurant employees work can lead to very circumscribed lifestyles for their wives and children as well as for themselves. Such information is invaluable to nurses and health visitors caring for Chinese families who may be reluctant to voice family health concerns. It is also important in that little has been written about the nursing needs of Britain's Chinese population, Goodbourn's (1987) article being one of the very few to be found in a nursing journal.

Among those in the forefront with innovative ideas for improving the health care offered to ethnic/cultural minorities are organizations such as the Save the Children Fund, which has been responsible for setting up mobile health clinics for gypsy/travelling families (e.g. Self, 1982), and also for launching an anti-rickets campaign directed towards the Asian community by Veena Bahl (1981), a nurse/health visitor. In addition, several health authorities in London, such as Hackney (Watson, 1984) and Bloomsbury (Bowen and Davey, 1986), and towns and cities elsewhere in the United Kingdom, have developed client advocacy schemes and employed ethnic minority clinic staff to work specifically with local ethnic minority communities in an effort to

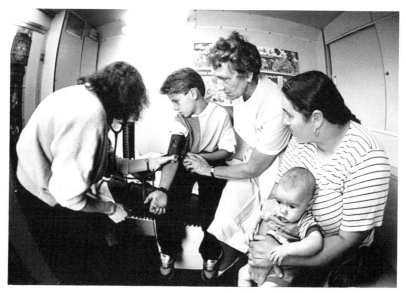

Fig. 11   Dr. Lesley Neal and health visitor Anne Eckford at their mobile
clinic during a visit to a travellers' site in Sheffield

bridge intercultural communication barriers for both
clients and health professionals.

It may be that in the United Kingdom multicultural/
transcultural nursing will develop closely and overtly in
tandem with multiracial nursing, the contemporary nursing
literature regularly addressing multiracial issues when
discussing multicultural concerns. Nurses (e.g. Pearson,
1986a and b) and others (e.g. Satow and Homans, 1982) have
been active in alerting the nursing profession to the presence of racial prejudice and to covert as well as overt racial
discrimination both within the profession and in the delivery of health care in general. However, terms such as
'ethnic people of colour' and 'visible minorities' have not
become part of the vocabulary used by nursing in the United
Kingdom in regard to racial minority groups as they have in
North America. As cutbacks force the nursing profession to
reconsider its approaches to promoting the nation's health
with reduced resources, including fewer nurses (e.g. Goodwin, 1988), the development and sustaining of racially as

well as culturally-sensitive nursing care may become even more imperilled than it has hitherto, and at a time when it has begun to take on wider and clearer dimensions.

As yet, there has been minimal conceptual development of intercultural nursing in the context of the United Kingdom. The two main contributions to conceptual development in contemporary British nursing are Roper, Logan and Tierney's (1990: 98) model for nursing practice and Clark's (1985; 1986) model for health visiting. Roper, Logan and Tierney's model includes sociocultural factors among those to be considered in relation to the client's activities of living. In contrast, Clark's model for health visiting, a model that is based in part on Neuman's model, lacks an explicit statement as to the importance of cultural factors. Concerned that nurses should look at their role in social rather than in traditional organizational terms, Keyzer (1986) recommends that frameworks for nursing practice should be based both on cultural concepts of care and on priorities for care as perceived by the client population rather than by the nursing profession. Although Keyzer (1986: 193) sees conceptual frameworks developed by North American nurses as useful to nurses in Britain, he nevertheless views the clinical nurse as ideally placed 'to gather information which, when collated, can lead to the creation of a "grounded" theory of nursing which reflects British nursing in its social, cultural and organisational setting'.

If the registered as well as the student nurse is to become proficient in nursing interculturally, then post-basic as well as basic nurse education must include a relevant knowledge base and adequate and appropriate practical experience. Burrows (1983) emphasized the need for the inclusion of ethnographic perspectives within nursing curricula in order that nurses themselves might learn to discover and understand the client's cultural world. Burrows' article is a significant watershed within the British nursing literature in that Burrows not only challenges the ethnocentricity of British nurse education, but discusses various ways in which a foundation of anthropological knowledge might be included within nurse education. Providing a succinct overview of various approaches advocated by differing

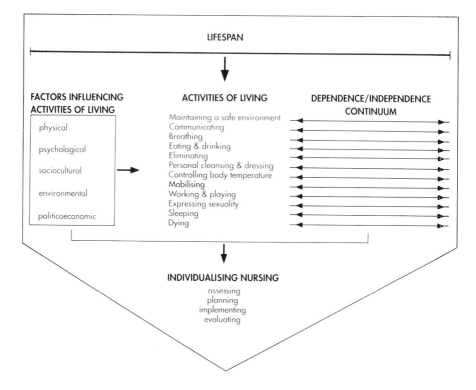

Fig. 12   Roper, Logan, Tierney (RLT) model

North American nurse educators, Burrows considers that rather than adhering to one single strategy when developing cultural content in nursing curricula:

> A combination of strategies is probably preferable, so that a broad anthropological knowledge foundation is provided and followed throughout the course by reference to cultural dimensions as a curriculum thread. (ibid.: 484)

She suggests that the exclusion of multicultural perspectives in nursing curricula represents a form of institutional racism. She also suggests that steps should be taken towards eliminating the existence of racial prejudice which is anathema to qualities, such as empathy and respect, inherent in the helping relationship so crucial to nursing practice (ibid.: 478). As more British nurses choose to nurse in countries within the European Community, the cultural content in nursing curricula will need to address the various European cultures (ibid.: 480), and the health needs and concerns of immigrants and migrants in European countries.

In a booklet entitled *Ethnic Minority Groups*, Sharman (1985) presents a number of issues for discussion when cultural and racial content in health visiting curricula is being planned. She raises the question of whether the content should be delivered within a separate and 'identifiable unit of learning' (ibid.: 6). While such a unit would be 'observable' and 'could be taught by members of minority groups themselves', a disadvantage might be that it

> would have connotations which imply that ethnic minority groups are a problem rather than accepting that in a multi-racial and multi-cultural society, all groups and their specific needs should be a natural part of the curriculum. (ibid.: 6–7)

Should an integrated approach be selected, then Sharman suggests (ibid.: 7) a need for caution lest lecturers teach about the dominant culture to the exclusion of minority cultures.

Although Sharman provides a variety of topics concerning race and culture needing to be addressed within the different subject areas covered by the health visiting syllabus, she fails to include the relevance of anthropological knowledge and insights, despite making specific reference to academic disciplines such as psychology and sociology (ibid.: 7). Indeed, the contribution that anthropological knowledge can provide to multicultural/transcultural nursing in the United Kingdom has been acknowledged only very recently, both by nurses and by British anthropologists. Articles such as Littlewood's (1988) entitled 'The Patient's World', and the founding of the Association of Nursing and Anthropology in 1986 (HV, 1986), are two instances of the relevance of anthropological knowledge and insights becoming better known to British nurses.

NURSING AND ANTHROPOLOGY

We have already seen how transcultural nursing arose from Leininger's initial interest in culture shaping client/patient behaviour and her realization that anthropological knowledge and insights could help her as a nurse to become better able to provide culturally astute care. Focusing on 'the holistic study of human beings from universal norms to individual idiosyncratic behaviors' (Brink, 1984: 111), anthropology offers a range of information about human behaviour not available from any other single discipline. While anthropology is concerned 'with holistically analyzing the place of humans in society and in nature', it is 'also, and especially' concerned 'with the way humans construct cultural frameworks in order to render their lives meaningful' (Peacock, 1986: 17). To the anthropologist, each individual 'is a cultural individual – existing in freedom but also embodying that cultural mold in which he is cast in his particular society and historical epoch' (ibid.: 46). Nursing is also concerned with the holistic concept of humankind and with people as cultural beings. Indeed, Leininger (1970: 1), in her book *Nursing and Anthropology*: Two Worlds to blend, questions why nurses and anthropologists have not previously 'shared their special insights, theoretical interests, and practical skills with one another'.

While anthropology has much to offer nursing, it is by no means the only academic discipline with a knowledge base that is of value to nurses to assist them in providing culturally relevant, client-centred care. Other social sciences concerned with the structure of society and with human behaviour and its variations, such as sociology (e.g. Theodore, 1989) and social psychology, are also important (Leininger, 1978: 57). Although each has its own particular point of view, the subject interest of sociology, social psychology and anthropology does overlap, such that it can be difficult at times to 'draw a clear line of demarcation between them' (Kakar and Dean, 1982: 36). In different countries academic disciplines may develop along somewhat different lines. Variations exist: the American anthropologist speaks of cultural anthropology, while the British anthropologist uses the term social anthropology. In an article concerning medical anthropology in North America and in the United Kingdom, Kaufert and Kaufert (1978) discuss at some length the divergent ways in which British and American anthropology have developed, and the differences in the relationship which each 'maintains with other disciplines, particularly with medical sociology' (ibid.: 255). Viewing medical sociology and medical anthropology as complementary, Foster (1978: 10) considers 'the anthropologist, consciously and subconsciously' as seeing 'problems and data in a cultural context, while the sociologist sees them in a social context'. It is this emphasis on culture as well as on holism that has resulted in anthropology, rather than sociology, being considered especially relevant to the development of transcultural nursing in North America. Leininger (1984b: 72) describes transcultural nursing as reflecting the 'synthesis of selected knowledge from anthropology and nursing'.

As a nurse-educator and nurse-anthropologist, Brink (1984: 132) observes that nurses who have worked with patients from cultures different from their own, and who have experienced frustration when their nursing care was attenuated by cultural constraints, have little trouble in seeing how anthropological theories and methods have relevance to nursing and the problems that occur in intercultural situations. Having an in-depth knowledge of both anthropology and nursing, the nurse-anthropologist is able to help student nurses see the relevance of anthropology to nursing practice, which, having little nursing experience, they might not see on their own. The nurse-anthropologist has the depth of insight into the problems nurses deal with in the various settings in which they function. Indeed, Chrisman (1982) writes at some length on his experiences as a non-nurse anthropologist in developing and presenting a cross-cultural programme, *Cultural Variation and Nursing Practice*. He found he needed to listen carefully to colleagues and students in order to discover 'what problems nurses face and were interested in solving' (ibid.: 129). Only then did he feel able to offer 'anthropology *in* nursing' rather than 'anthropology *and* nursing' (ibid.: 128).

Being 'inherently pragmatic' (Brink, 1984: 108) and often

needing to solve immediate problems, nurses require cultural information that is relevant to the type of situations
they face and the problems and dilemmas with which they
must cope. Although the ideas and findings of medical
anthropologists are often pertinent and useful to nursing,
they are seldom linked to nursing-specific problems and
situations. Helman's (1985) *Culture, Health and Illness* and
Landy's (1977) edited text *Culture, Disease, and Healing* are
two examples of important works in medical anthropology,
which reveal little acquaintance by medical anthropologists
with publications by nurses, including those by nurse-
anthropologists. However, the collated proceedings from
the National Transcultural Nursing conferences held by the
Transcultural Nursing Society (e.g. Leininger, 1979),
together with articles published in various nursing journals
such as the *Journal of Transcultural Nursing*, form useful
sources of research findings and discussion which provide
other nurses with an indication of the scope of concerns that
nurse-anthropologists are addressing.

Tripp-Reimer (1985) links anthropological concepts with
the four concepts or elements: society/environment, humans,
health and nursing, which together form the domain of
nursing. She describes the contribution that she sees anthropology providing to the expansion of each of the four
concepts, and thus to nursing theory. To the conceptualization of society/environment, Tripp-Reimer sees anthropology as contributing the concept of culture. The nurse needs
to be cognisant of his/her own cultural beliefs, values and
behaviours as well as those of the client. Both client and
nurse 'exist and interact in a cultural milieu' (Tripp-Reimer,
1985: 92). Anthropology provides the concepts of ethnocentrism and cultural relativity to the conceptualization of
humans, each concept being a side of 'the same coin', for the
distinction between each concerns whether the data that
nurses collect 'are interpreted from the perspective of the
client or that of the nurse' (ibid.: 94).

> From an ethnocentric perspective, nurses judge the behavior of
> a client of a different culture from the standards of their own.
> From a cultural relativist perspective, the caregiver attempts to

understand the behavior of clients within the context of the client's culture. (ibid.: 94)

For the expansion of the concept of health, Tripp-Reimer offers a health grid, which she devised and presents at length in another publication (Tripp-Reimer, 1984). This grid (see also Chapter 4, page 112) utilizes the emic–etic distinction derived from anthropology, the emic approach yielding 'a description of a cultural system from the inside' or how the members of the culture see it, while the etic analysis 'consists of observing behavior without learning the viewpoint of those studied' (ibid.: 103). This health grid comprises two axes, the vertical axis being an illness–wellness continuum, the horizontal axis a disease–non-disease continuum. The former is the emic category which represents the client's perspective, while the other is the etic category representing the biomedical perspective which Tripp-Reimer (1985: 95) considers to have 'units of analysis' which 'can be applied universally across cultures'. Finally, she sees the concept of culture-broker as derived from the discipline of anthropology as extending the concept of nursing, culture brokerage being viewed as a nursing intervention which she and Brink expand further in another publication (Tripp-Reimer and Brink, 1985). As a nursing intervention, cultural brokerage is seen to involve 'the nurse acting as a mediator' between clients (e.g. ethnic minority clients) and orthodox health professionals, and 'may focus on the client, on the health professional, or on mediation between both' (Tripp-Reimer, 1985: 98–9).

Nurse-anthropologists, of whom there are now a substantial number in North America, have been active in promoting transcultural nursing throughout Canada and the United States. They have provided anthropology with an area of concern that had previously been minimally explored, even within the ambit of medical anthropology. Such developments are only now beginning to emerge in Britain, and it may be that transcultural nursing in Britain will develop along a somewhat different path from the one transcultural nursing has taken in North America. Littlewood (1988: 30), for instance, sees transcultural nursing in

North America as having developed the idea of a nurse who is an 'expert' for a particular culture, a situation which she views negatively in that she considers that this has resulted in 'white American nurses' distancing themselves from their patients, their approach becoming 'blinded' as a result.

REFERENCES

International Nursing Foundation of Japan (1977) *Nursing in the World. The needs of individual countries, and their programmes*, ed. Nursing in the World editorial committee. Tokyo: International Nursing Foundation of Japan.

United States of America and Canada – Transcultural Nursing

Aamodt AM (1978) Culture. In AL Clark (ed.), *Culture, Childbearing, Health Professionals*. Philadelphia: Davis.
Aamodt AM (1981) Neighboring. Discovering support systems among Norwegian–American women. In DA Messerschmidt (ed.), *Anthropologists at Home in North America. Methods and issues in the study of one's own society*. New York: Cambridge University Press.
Aichlmayr RH (1969) Cultural understanding. A key to acceptance. *Nursing Outlook* **17**(7): 20–3.
Baker CM and Mayer GG (1982) One approach to teaching cultural similarities and differences. *Journal of Nursing Education* **21**(4): 17–22.
Bonaparte BH (1979) Ego defensiveness, open-closed mindedness, and nurses' attitude toward culturally different patients. *Nursing Research* **28**(3): 166–72.
Boyle JS and Andrews MM (eds) (1989) *Transcultural Concepts in Nursing Care*. Glenview, IL: Scott, Foresman.
Branch MF and Paxton PP (1976) *Providing Safe Nursing Care for Ethnic People of Color*. New York: Appleton-Century-Crofts.
Brink PJ (1984) Key issues in nursing and anthropology. *Advances in Medical Social Science* **2**: 107–46.
Brown EL (1948) *Nursing for the Future*. New York: Russell Sage.

Brown EL (1964) *Newer Dimensions of Patient Care.* Part 3. *Patients as People.* New York: Russell Sage.

Burrows A (1983) Patient-centred nursing care in a multi-racial society. The relevance of ethnographic perspectives in nursing curricula. *Journal of Advanced Nursing* 8(6): 477–85.

Byerly EL (1977) Cultural components in the baccalaureate nursing curriculum. Philosophy, goals and processes. In *Cultural Dimensions in the Baccalaureate Nursing Curriculum.* New York: National League for Nursing.

Carpio B (1981) The adolescent immigrant. *Canadian Nurse* 77(3): 27, 30–1.

Chrisman NJ (1982) Anthropology in nursing. An exploration of adaptation. In NJ Chrisman and TW Maretzki (eds), *Clinically Applied Anthropology. Anthropologists in health science settings.* Dordrecht: Reidel.

Clausen JP (1978) Cancer diagnoses in children. Cultural factors influencing parent/child reactions. *Cancer Nursing* 1(5): 395–401.

Davies M and Yoshida M (1981) A model for cultural assessment of the new immigrant. *Canadian Nurse* 77(3): 22–3.

Davis MM and Haasis BA (1920) The visiting nurse and the immigrant. *The Public Health Nurse* 12: 823–34.

DeSantis L (1988) The relevance of transcultural nursing to international nursing. *International Nursing Review* 35(4): 110–12, 116.

Dougherty MC and Tripp-Reimer T (1985) The interface of nursing and anthropology. *Annual Review of Anthropology* 14: 219–41.

Fulton C (1985) Integrating cultural content into the nursing curriculum. *Nurse Educator* 10(1): 26–31.

Garner VM and Merrill E (1976) A model for development and implementation of cultural content in the nursing curriculum. *Journal of Nursing Education* 15(2): 30–4.

Germain CP (1982) Cultural concepts in critical care. *Critical Care Quarterly* 5(3): 61–78.

Glasgow JM and Adaskin EJ (1990) The West Indians. In N Waxler-Morrison, JM Anderson and E Richardson (eds), *Cross-cultural caring: a handbook for health professionals in western Canada.* Vancouver: University of British Columbia Press.

Hodgson C (1980) Transcultural nursing. The Canadian experience. *Canadian Nurse* 76(6): 23–5.

Jaffe Ruiz MC (1981) Open-closed mindedness, intolerance of ambiguity and nursing faculty attitudes toward culturally different patients. *Nursing Research* 30(3): 177–81.

Kapsa CW (1989) Organ transplants. Cultural issues and moral problems. In JS Boyle and MM Andrews (eds), *Transcultural Concepts in Nursing Care*. Glenview, IL: Scott, Foresman.

King IM (1981) *A Theory for Nursing. Systems, concepts, process.* New York: John Wiley.

Koshi PT (1976) Cultural diversity in the nursing curricula. *Journal of Nursing Education* 15(2): 14–21.

Laughlin A (1989) Smiles are all part of the treatment at the Children's. *The Gazette* [Montreal], 30 June, p. J1.

Leininger M (ed.) (1978) *Transcultural Nursing. Concepts, theories, and practices.* New York: John Wiley.

Leininger M (1979) *Principles and Guidelines to Assist Nurses in Cross-cultural Nursing and Health Practices.* Paper presented at the International Nursing Conference sponsored by Project HOPE, and held at Project HOPE Health Sciences Education Center, Millwood, VA, 16–19 September.

Leininger M (1981) The phenomenon of caring. Importance, research questions and theoretical considerations. In *Caring. An essential human need.* Thorofare, NJ: Slack.

Leininger M (1984a) Transcultural interviewing and health assessment. In PB Pedersen, N Sartorius and AJ Marsella (eds), *Mental Health Services. The cross-cultural context.* Beverly Hills, CA: Sage.

Leininger M (1984b) Transcultural nursing. An overview. *Nursing Outlook* 32(2): 72–3.

Leininger M (1985) Transcultural care diversity and universality. A theory of nursing. *Nursing and Health Care* 6(4): 208–12.

Leininger M (1988) Leininger's theory of nursing: Cultural care diversity and universality. *Nursing Science Quarterly* 1(4): 152–60.

Lipson JG (1988) The cultural perspective in nursing education. *Practicing Anthropology* 10(2): 4–5.

Ludwig-Beymer P (1989) Transcultural aspects of pain. In JS Boyle and MM Andrews (eds), *Transcultural Concepts in Nursing Care*. Glenview, IL: Scott, Foresman.

MacDonald J (1987) Preparing to work in a multicultural society. *Canadian Nurse* 83(8): 31–2.

Macgregor FC (1960) *Social Science in Nursing*. New York: Russell Sage.

Mattson S (1987) The need for cultural concepts in nursing curricula. *Journal of Nursing Education* 26(5): 206–8.

Morgan BS (1983) Selected correlates of white nursing students' attitudes toward black American patients. *International Journal of Nursing Studies* 20(2): 109–21.

Murillo-Rohde I (1978) Cultural diversity in curriculum development. In M Leininger (ed.), *Transcultural Nursing. Concepts, theories, and practices.* New York: John Wiley.

Neuman B (1985) The Neuman systems model. *Senior Nurse* 3(3): 20–3.

Orem DE (1985) *Nursing. Concepts of practice.* New York: McGraw-Hill.

Orque MS (1981) Cultural components. In MD Jensen, RC Benson and IM Bobak (eds), *Maternity Care. The nurse and the family,* 2nd edn. St Louis: CV Mosby.

Orque MS (1983) Orque's ethnic/cultural system. A framework for ethnic nursing care. In MS Orque, B Bloch and LSA Monrroy (eds), *Ethnic Nursing Care. A multicultural approach.* St Louis: CV Mosby.

Orque MS, Bloch B and Monrroy LSA (eds) (1983) *Ethnic Nursing Care. A multicultural approach.* St Louis: CV Mosby.

Ragucci AT (1971) *Generational Continuity and Change in Concepts of Health, Curing Practices, and Ritual Expressions of the Women of an Italian–American Enclave.* Unpublished PhD dissertation, Boston University, MA.

Ragucci AT (1972) The ethnographic approach and nursing research. *Nursing Research* 21(6): 485–90.

Satz KJ (1982) Integrating Navajo tradition into maternal–child nursing. *Image* 14(3): 89–91.

Sohier R (1989) Nursing care for the people of a small planet. Culture and the Neuman systems model. In B Neuman (ed.), *The Neuman Systems Model,* 2nd edn. Norwalk, CT: Appleton & Lange.

Spector RE (1979) *Cultural Diversity in Health and Illness.* New York: Appleton-Century-Crofts.

Tripp-Reimer T (1983) Retention of a folk-healing practice (*matiasma*) among four generations of urban Greek immigrants. *Nursing Research* 32(2): 97–101.

Tripp-Reimer T (1984a) Cultural assessment. In JP Bellack and PA Bamford (eds), *Nursing Assessment. A multidimensional approach.* Monterey, CA: Wadsworth.

Tripp-Reimer T (1984b) Research in cultural diversity. Directions for future research. *Western Journal of Nursing Research* 6(2): 253–5.

Wald LD (1915) *The House on Henry Street.* New York: Holt & Co.

Yoshida M and Davies M (1985) An innovative project – childbearing and childrearing: Recent immigrant families in the urban Toronto setting. In M Stewart, J Innes, S Searl and C Smillie (eds), *Community Health Nursing in Canada.* Toronto: Gage.

United Kingdom – Multicultural Nursing

Abbas V (1981) *A Theoretical Examination of the Factors Involved in Health Education with Ethnic Minority Groups.* Unpublished dissertation submitted for the Diploma in Health Education, University of Leeds.

Alexander B (1974) Help for immigrant families. *Nursing Times* **70**(17): 632–6.

Anionwu E and Beattie A (1981) Learning to cope with sickle cell disease. A parent's experience. *Nursing Times* **77**(28): 1214–19.

Attariwala R (1977) Asian children and school meals in the UK. A question of choice. *Journal of Human Nutrition* **31**(4): 251–5.

Ayekoto S (1972) Let's all work together. *Nursing Mirror* **134**(25): 8.

Bahl V (1981) Stop rickets campaign. *Nutrition and Food Science*, May/June, No. 70: 2–5.

Ballard R (1979) Ethnic minorities and the social services. What type of service? In V Saifullah Khan (ed.), *Minority Families in Britain. Support and stress.* London: Macmillan.

Bhaduri R (1979) A family's sorrow. *Nursing Times* **75**(15): 638–9.

Bowen E and Davey E (1986) Assessment of the use of Bengali health aides. *Midwives Chronicle and Nursing Notes* **99**(1180): 102–4.

Bunting A (1984) Asian women and contraception. *Senior Nurse* **1**(29): 12, 14, 16.

Burrows A (1983) Patient-centred nursing care in a multi-racial society. The relevance of ethnographic perspectives in nursing curricula. *Journal of Advanced Nursing* **8**(6): 477–85.

Carlisle D (1990) Racism in nursing. *Nursing Times* **86**(14): 25–7,29.

Clark J (1985) *The Process of Health Visiting.* Unpublished PhD thesis, Council for National Academic Awards. London: Polytechnic of the South Bank.

Clark J (1986) A model for health visiting. In B Kershaw and J Salvage (eds), *Models for Nursing.* Chichester: John Wiley.

Clark J and Henderson J (eds) (1983) *Community Health.* Edinburgh: Churchill Livingstone.

Coombe V (1976) Health and social services and minority ethnic groups. *Journal of the Royal Society of Health* **96**(1): 34–8.

CRE (Commission for Racial Equality) (1976) *Afro Hair, Skin Care and Recipes.* London: CRE.

CRE (Commission for Racial Equality) (1977) *A Home from Home? Some policy considerations on black children in residential care.* London: CRE.

Crow J (1977) Nursing care using a care plan. In *The Nursing Process*. London: Macmillan.

Davie E (1979) The cultural dimension. *Community Care*, No. 264: 36–9.

Davitz LL and Davitz JR (1985) Culture and nurses' inferences of suffering. *Recent Advances in Nursing* [Perspectives on pain] 11, ed. LA Copp.

DHSS (Department of Health and Social Security) (1984) *Services for under Fives from Ethnic Minority Communities*. Report of a sub-group on provision of services for under fives from ethnic minority communities. London: HMSO.

Dunnigan MG, McIntosh WB, Sutherland GR, Gardee R, Glekin B, Ford JA and Robertson I (1981) Policy for prevention of Asian rickets in Britain. A preliminary assessment of the Glasgow rickets campaign. *British Medical Journal* 282: 357–60.

Dwivedi KN (1980) Indian notions in counselling situations. *Counselling News*, May, No. 32: 10–14.

Ellis S (1978) That unspoken prejudice. *Nursing Times* 74(48): 1964–5.

Fuller JHS and Toon PD (1988) *Medical Practice in a Multicultural Society*. Oxford: Heinemann.

Goodbourn P (1987) Health for all – the Chinese, too. *Focus* 9: 8–9.

Goodwin S (1988) Whither health visiting? *Health Visitor* 61(12): 379–83.

Griffin AM (1972) Understanding the immigrant worker. *Occupational Health* 24(4): 121–7.

HEC (Health Education Council/National Extension College) (1984) *Black Health Workers*. Report of a one-day seminar for black professional health workers held in London on 19 November 1983. London: Health Education Council/National Extension College for Training in Health and Race.

Helman C (1985) *Culture, Health and Illness. An introduction for health professionals*. Bristol: Wright.

Henley A (1979) *Asian Patients in Hospital and at Home*. London: King Edward's Hospital Fund for London.

Homans H (1982) Pregnancy and birth as rites of passage for two groups of women in Britain. In CP MacCormack (ed.), *Ethnography of Fertility and Birth*. London: Academic Press.

HV (Health Visitor) (1986) Anthropology and primary health care. *Health Visitor* 59(9): 268.

Illing M and Donovan B (1981) *District Nursing*. London: Baillière Tindall.

Karseras P (1988) Ignorance, poverty and health care. *Health Visitor* 61(9): 282.

Karseras P and Hopkins E (1987) *British Asians: Health in the Community*. Chichester: John Wiley.

Keyzer D (1986) Concepts of care. A way of life. *Nursing Practice* **1:** 190–5.

Kitzinger S (1977) Challenges in antenatal education. 1. Immigrant women in childbirth – an anthropologist's view. *Nursing Mirror* **144**(25): 19–22.

Knight L (1978) Protect their minds too. *Mind Out* **31,** Nov.–Dec., 12–14.

Lam E (1980) Health visiting Vietnamese refugees in Britain. *Health Visitor* **53:** 254–5.

LCRC (Lothian Community Relations Council) (1983) *Needs of the Chinese Community in Lothian*. A report based on a study by E Chan. Edinburgh: Lothian Community Relations Council.

Littlewood J (1988) The patient's world. *Nursing Times* **84**(3): 29–30.

Littlewood R and Lipsedge M (1982) *Aliens and Alienists. Ethnic minorities and psychiatry*. Harmondsworth: Penguin Books.

Lobo E de H (1978) *Children of Immigrants to Britain. Their health and social problems*. London: Hodder & Stoughton.

Mares P (1982) *The Vietnamese in Britain. A handbook for health workers*. Cambridge: Health Education Council/National Extension College.

Mares P, Henley A and Baxter C (1985) *Health Care in Multiracial Britain*. Cambridge: Health Education Council/National Extension College.

May A and Choiseul M (1988) Sickle cell anaemia and thalassaemia. Symptoms, treatment and effects on lifestyle. *Health Visitor* **61**(7): 212–15.

Moore J (1984) Out in the cold. *Nursing Times* **80**(30): 19–20.

Nightingale F (1894) Health teaching in towns and villages. Rural hygiene. In *Selected Writings of Florence Nightingale* (1954), comp. LR Seymer. New York: Macmillan.

Pearson M (1986a) Ten years on. *Senior Nurse* **4**(4): 18–19.

Pearson M (1986b) Less favourable treatment? *Senior Nurse* **4**(5): 15–17.

Pearson R (1982) Understanding Vietnamese in Britain. Part 1: Background and family life. *Health Visitor* **55**(8): 426–7, 429–30.

Qureshi B (1985) Obstetric problems in multi-ethnic women. *Maternal and Child Health* **10**(10): 303–7.

Qureshi B (1989) *Transcultural Medicine. Dealing with Patients from Different Cultures*. Dordrecht: Kluwer Academic.

Rack P (1982) *Race, Culture, and Mental Disorder*. London: Tavistock.

Roper N, Logan WW and Tierney AJ (1990) *The Elements of Nursing. A Model for Nursing based on a Model for Living.* 3rd edn. Edinburgh: Churchill Livingstone.

Sampson C (1982) *The Neglected Ethic. Religious and cultural factors in the care of patients.* Maidenhead: McGraw-Hill.

Satow A and Homans H (1982) Fair service for all. *Journal of Community Nursing*, February, **5**(8): 19, 21–2.

Self J (1982) 'Will you weigh m'baby, lady?' *Nursing Times* **78**(39): 1620–4.

Sharman RL (1985) *Ethnic Minority Groups. A discussion paper on curriculum development in health visiting.* London: English National Board for Nursing, Midwifery and Health Visiting.

Turrell S (1985) Asian expectations. *Nursing Times* **81**(18): 44–6.

University of Manchester (1981) *Health Care Provision for the Asian Community.* Working paper No. 45, Health Services Management Unit, Dept of Social Administration, University of Manchester.

Watson C (1984) The vital link. *Nursing Times* **80**(30): 18–19.

Wilson G (1988) On the road. *Nursing Times* **84**(3): 26–7.

Nursing and Anthropology

Brink PJ (1984) Key issues in nursing and anthropology. *Advances in Medical Social Science* **2**: 107–46.

Chrisman NJ (1982) Anthropology in nursing. An exploration of adaptation. In NJ Chrisman and TW Maretzki (eds), *Clinically Applied Anthropology. Anthropologists in health science settings.* Dordrecht: Reidel.

Foster GM (1978) Medical anthropology: some contrasts with medical sociology. In MH Logan and EE Hunt (eds), *Health and the Human Condition. Perspectives on medical anthropology.* North Scituate, MA: Duxbury Press.

Helman C (1985) *Culture, Health and Illness. An introduction for health professionals.* Bristol: Wright.

Kakar DN and Dean M (1982) Social science in nursing education and research. *Nursing Journal of India* **73**(2): 35–6.

Kaufert PL and Kaufert JM (1978) Alternate courses of development. Medical anthropology in Britain and North America. *Social Science and Medicine* **12B**: 255–61.

Landy D (ed) (1977) *Culture, Disease, and Healing. Studies in medical anthropology.* New York: Macmillan.

Leininger M (1970) *Nursing and Anthropology. Two worlds to blend.* New York: John Wiley.

Leininger M (ed.) (1978) *Transcultural Nursing. Concepts, theories, and practices*. New York: John Wiley.

Leininger M (ed.) (1979) *Transcultural Nursing '79*. Proceedings of the National Transcultural Nursing conferences. New York: Masson.

Leininger M (1984b) Transcultural nursing. An overview. *Nursing Outlook* **32**(2): 72–3.

Littlewood J (1988) The patient's world. *Nursing Times* **84**(3): 29–30.

Peacock JL (1986) *The Anthropological Lens. Harsh light, soft focus*. Cambridge: Cambridge University Press.

Theodore J (1989) Sociology by any other name. *Nursing Times* **85**(19); 74–5.

Tripp-Reimer T (1984) Reconceptualizing the construct of health. Integrating emic and etic perspectives. *Research in Nursing and Health* **7**(2): 101–9.

Tripp-Reimer T (1985) Expanding four essential concepts in nursing theory. The contribution of anthropology. In JC McCloskey and HK Grace (eds), *Current Issues in Nursing*, 2nd edn. Boston, MA: Blackwell.

Tripp-Reimer T and Brink PJ (1985) Culture brokerage. In GM Bulechek and JC McCloskey (eds), *Nursing Interventions. Treatments for nursing diagnoses*. Philadelphia: Saunders.

CHAPTER 4

Cultural Discovery for Nursing Practice

Having looked at the development of transcultural nursing, including the contribution that nurse anthropologists have provided to raising nurses' awareness of the relevance of culture to nursing care, in this chapter we look at the nursing process in some depth. In so doing, emphasis is given to the assessment stage, the findings of which form the basis from which the other three stages proceed. Cultural factors are given prominence. Then a number of cultural assessment guides are described, some of which have a specific focus and each its own approach to the collection and collation of cultural information.

The need for nurses to develop proficiency in discovering and using cultural information is highlighted in the final section. The idea of a 'mini-' or attenuated ethnography is presented as one approach to nurses developing expertise in cultural discovery – expertise that will allow them to diagnose with greater cultural accuracy and deliver nursing care in a more culturally relevant and sensitive manner in intercultural situations. It is suggested that a small-scale ethnographic study might be incorporated into basic and continuing nurse education with a view to nurses using ethnographic approaches to cultural discovery in their everyday practice, whether they practise in hospitals, nursing homes, industrial workplaces or in the community.

THE NURSING PROCESS

In many countries, the nursing process is used as an organized, systematic approach to assessing client needs and to planning and implementing thoughtful and thorough nursing care. Though frequently depicted as a circle, the process invariably assumes spiralling dimensions, nursing care usually being an ongoing activity constantly under revision, building on what has preceded. Beginning with assessment (data collection, analysis and diagnosis), the process leads on to the planning and implementation of nursing care, and thereafter to the evaluation of care provided by the nurse and/or undertaken by the client and the client's significant others. In some situations, a nursing contract between nurse and client is used, emphasizing the shared nature of nursing care (Spradley, 1981a: 133–46). Although important, cultural factors are seldom discussed in the literature as they relate to each stage of the nursing process, notable exceptions being publications by Orque, Bloch and Monrroy (1983), Boyle and Andrews (1989a) and Littlewood (1989).

Guided by the particular concerns and hopes the client presents, and drawing on previous knowledge and clinical experience, the nurse must decide what questions to ask and what to observe. As the findings of the assessment stage act as a foundation for the planning and implementation of nursing care, relevant, accurate and sufficient cultural information is essential. During the assessment stage, the nurse coalesces and re-coalesces subjective and objective information, looking for significant patterns within the data which point to possible diagnoses. Whenever feasible, inferences made are validated with the client and/or his/her significant others. The nursing diagnosis is, or should be, a statement that reflects accurately the client's health state, and may be problem- or wellness-oriented (e.g. Houldin, Saltstein and Ganley, 1987). Plans are then drawn up and implemented, goals being mutually determined and, again, involving significant others as appropriate. Precise behavioural objectives provide a clear basis for subsequent evaluation: what, for example, will be done, who will do it and when will it be accomplished? Perhaps the mother of a London Chinese family will introduce *congee*, which the nurse has discovered is a traditional Chinese weaning food (Tann and Wheeler, 1980: 21–2), into the diet of her six-month-old infant while continuing to breast-feed. Subsequently, mother and nurse determine whether the outcomes achieved were those hoped for. Has the introduction of *congee* helped to sustain the infant for longer periods of the day than breast-milk alone was achieving? Careful documentation is also important, Ismail's World (Rhodes, 1980) being an example, in article form, of the nursing process in use in relation to the care of a Pakistani Muslim child.

While it is especially important that cultural information be included in the initial assessment stage in order that a culturally relevant and accurate diagnosis is reached, cultural information is important to all subsequent stages: planning, implementation and evaluation. As the nurse becomes increasingly more experienced in caring for clients from various cultures, s/he develops a 'cerebral library' (Carnevali, 1983: 56) of pertinent cultural information which allows him/her to move through the various stages of the nursing process with increased cultural adroitness. The nurse has learnt what types of question will lead to significant cultural information in various situations among certain cultural groups without having to spend inordinate amounts of time pursuing inappropriate avenues of enquiry, a time-consuming activity for both client and nurse. In addition, the nurse has developed insight into what are acceptable ways to approach a problem in a particular culture and what topics may be discussed with whom.

Before moving on to consider the diagnostic process in more detail and, briefly, the other stages of the nursing process, let us first look at several factors relevant to the use of the nursing process in intercultural situations.

General Considerations

When using the nursing process in conjunction with one of the many recognized conceptual frameworks or models for nursing practice currently available (e.g. Roper, Logan and

Tierney, 1990 [activities of living]; Yura and Walsh, 1988 [human needs]: see Aggleton and Chalmers, 1986), it is important that one is chosen that has relevance to the client's cultural orientation. Some models focus, for example, on the individual person, others on composite clientele such as the family (see e.g. Griffith-Kenney and Christensen, 1986). Others again allow for either an individualistic or a collectivistic orientation. As a member of an actively caring 'socio-cultural-religious network' (Andrews, 1989: 152), the Amish client may prefer to be considered within collectivist, or group, dimensions (Hofstede, 1980: 214–15). Among the Amish, certain non-blood members are considered relatives, and an individual's medical bill is paid for through shared communal resources (Andrews, 1989: 152). The Hutterite client, who is also a member of a socio-cultural-religious community, may also wish to be viewed and nursed within a collectivistic orientation (e.g. Hostetler and Huntington, 1970: 202–3).

Fig. 13   Hutterite children, Canada

Skilful and sensitive nurse–client communication lies at the heart of using the nursing process in transcultural nursing. In using the term 'transcultural' as opposed to 'intercultural', not only is the presence and the awareness of more than one culture in the nurse–client relationship implied, but also the co-existence of an affirmative desire on the part of the practitioner to bridge and transcend intercultural differences (Dobson, 1989: 99). If, indeed, nurses in intercultural situations are to provide advice, guidance and practical help in accord with the client's culture and, moreover, as the client sees this to be, then they must make affirmative efforts to emancipate themselves from their own cultural view and take a metaphorical step into their client's cultural world. Although many descriptions of the nursing process place the nurse in a dominant, management position, a sense of mutuality between client and nurse, a 'two-way sharing of information, ideas, feeling, concerns, and ultimately, self' (Spradley, 1981b: 100), should prevail. With cultural disparities between nurse and client usually being minimal in intracultural situations, the reciprocation of cultural knowledge and respect, or 'intra-cultural reciprocity' (Dobson, 1989: 101), can be considered to occur with minimal interference, although other personal and social differences may intrude. In intercultural situations, however, cultural differences need to be actively bridged and transcended if the reciprocation of cultural respect and knowledge, or 'transcultural reciprocity' (ibid.: 100–1), is to be established. While easy to advocate, the establishment of transcultural reciprocity may be far from easy to achieve, impeded at times by other factors such as racial or social class differences perceived by either client or nurse, or indeed both. If reciprocation of cultural knowledge and respect does not occur, for whatever reason, then the likelihood of culturally relevant care being provided will be reduced.

Far from being confined to situations in which nurses of the dominant culture care for ethnic minority clients, intercultural difficulties and misunderstandings may exist when nurse and client are from two different cultural minorities, or when an ethnic minority nurse cares for a

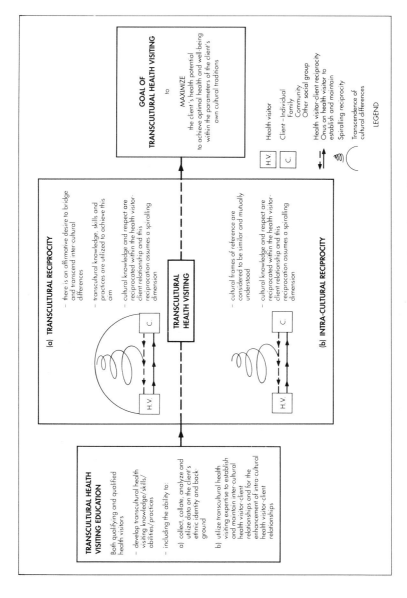

Fig. 14   Transcultural health visiting-schema—Dobson

client from the ethnic majority. Qureshi (1986: 438) offers examples of misunderstandings that may occur in various intercultural encounters, e.g. Italian-Vietnamese, Chinese-Polish and English-Indian health visitor–client interactions. Many a cultural misunderstanding or what may seem an impasse, if recognized as being culturally based, can be discussed and, if possible, quickly resolved. At times the nurse may find a particular cultural belief or practice unacceptable. Many health professionals find female circumcision unacceptable, but offering concerned and culturally sensitive care to the woman who has been circumcized is nevertheless imperative (see Brown, Calder and Rae, 1989).

Becoming sensitive to the ways and symbolism of another culture, to its logic and forms of etiquette, is seldom easy or straightforward. It requires a keen willingness to observe, listen to and learn from clients whose cultural backgrounds differ from one's own. Gregory (1988: 175) emphasizes the importance of nurses who work in rural and northern native communities in Canada being well-versed in the particular culture, be it native Indian, Inuit or Métis. Cardenas and Lucarz (1985) highlight the subtleties of communication required of community health nurses wishing to gain acceptance by the Cree Indian of Canada. Gaining acceptance is like entering a series of concentric circles, each circle representing 'ever-increasing approximation to the centre or core of the knowledge and understanding of Indian lifeways' (ibid.: 262). The new nurse, unfamiliar with Cree Indian ways, waits on the rim of the outer circle. The only way into the outer circle is, by analogy, through the traditional Indian tent, the *tipi*, which symbolizes core Indian values and the home and extended family within which these are traditionally learnt. Rather than directly sharing with the nurse the implications of customs and symbolism unique to his or her particular tribe and band, the Indian person waits for the nurse

> to discover the meaning through sensitive observation, active listening and experiencing the situation. Symbols and customs must be used by the nurse carefully and respectfully. The Indian person will quickly discern the authenticity of the gesture. (ibid.: 265)

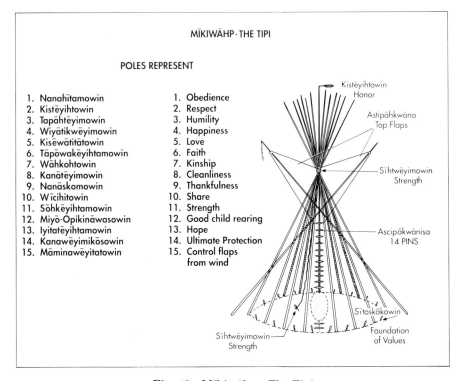

Fig. 15 Mīkiwāhp – The Tipi

Only little by little is the nurse permitted to enter each of the concentric circles. This hesitancy in permitting a nurse of another culture from becoming speedily acquainted with the group's cultural ways is in no way peculiar to the native Indian of Canada. Other cultural groups are also selective in admitting outsiders to share insights into their culture and acceptance into their cultural group.

Some clients may find it difficult to explain their cultural ways and beliefs to someone who has had little previous acquaintance with their culture, or if the client has emigrated from a country where life differs substantially from life in the receiving country. Sometimes clients are experiencing culture shock – an overwhelming sense of cultural dislocation and disorientation which, in all likelihood, would be magnified if they required hospitalization while still a new immigrant (see Brink and Saunders, 1976). A series of photographs contrasting village life in northern India with urban life in the United Kingdom portrays vividly some of the immense changes in lifestyle, which many Kashmiri families face on migration to Britain (Martin and Walsh, 1981). Other clients may be political refugees, who, in addition to an immense sense of cultural rift, may have memories of torture and persecution which they understandably may be reluctant to share with others (e.g. Allodi et al., 1986). At times, it will not be the client who is the newcomer to a country or locality, but the nurse who is learning to adjust to life among people whose culture is different from his/her own.

The manner in which information is elicited is another important factor to consider in client assessment. For each culture there are usual and acceptable ways of eliciting information. Among the Ojibway and Cree Indians of Canada, for instance, asking

> direct factual or personal questions violates Ojibway and Cree etiquette; the questioner is likely to be greeted with silence or, at the most, contentless or deflecting answers, which nurses may label a lack of cooperation or poor attitude. (Hagey and McDonough, 1984: 156)

Certain questions, because of the way in which they are phrased and/or delivered, may bear very different connotations for a client of one culture from those for a client of another and, indeed, be vastly different from those the nurse intended. Among the Bomvana of the Transkei in South Africa, about whom Jansen (1973: 167) writes, to intimate in any way that a child with primary tuberculosis has been infected by other members of the *kraal* is unacceptable. To do so is akin to implying that the members of the *kraal* are culpable for the sickness – an association which is conceived in terms of witchcraft.

Difficulties inherent in translating ideas and concepts developed within the language of one culture into that of another are well-known (e.g. Wright, 1953), and even when skilled interpreters are used, ideas can often be virtually impossible to translate with precision. Mares, Henley and Baxter (1985) and Fuller and Toon (1988) provide much useful advice about communicating across a language barrier and the use of interpreters. Non-verbal language, such as the use of facial expressions, silence, timing and spatial distances, can convey messages as important and powerful as those verbally conveyed, and often are culture-specific (Hall and Whyte, 1960). Culture also shapes the way in which humans express pain and suffering, and indeed how nurses interpret pain and suffering experienced by others (Davitz and Davitz, 1985).

Diagnostic Process – Cultural Aspects

Let us look now at one step of the nursing process, the diagnostic process, nursing diagnosis being the end-point of the assessment stage. If planning to use formal nursing diagnoses, such as those in the taxonomy compiled by the North American Nursing Diagnosis Association (NANDA; e.g. Kim, McFarland and McLane, 1989) the nurse must first decide how relevant certain diagnoses are to cultures worldwide (cf. Potter and Perry, 1987: 308). Can one refer to a knowledge deficit when a client adheres to a very different cultural logic from that on which Western medical science is based? Can one even consider knowledge deficit a valid diagnosis at all (Jenny, 1987)? Is the sick or disabled patient to whom dependence on family members is considered culturally acceptable, and indeed in some cultures expected, to be viewed as non-compliant if she or he is disinclined to make vast efforts to be rehabilitated along lines that the nursing or medical staff expect of them (LaFargue, 1980)?

As a process, diagnosing involves the nurse looking for patterns within the data, ultimately deciding '*this* . . . is an example of *that*' (King, 1967: 154), or at least he or she thinks it is. Whether or not the idea of nursing diagnosis *per se* is accepted (Hagey and McDonough (1984) and Mitchell and Santopinto (1988) being among those who caution against the use of standard nursing diagnoses), a decision is never-theless made as to what the problem or need is that nursing will address. Without cultural data, such a decision (or nursing diagnosis) cannot be adequately supported.

The diagnostic process, as described by Carnevali (1983: 45–61), comprises seven stages or elements, which form 'a potential pattern of use rather than rigid steps' (Carnevali 1984: 28; see also Dobson, 1988). These seven stages are:

1. pre-encounter (or pre-entry) influences,
2. entry into the data field,
3. developing cue clusters,
4. activation of possible diagnostic explanations,
5. directed data search,
6. evaluation of diagnostic possibilities,
7. assignment of a diagnostic label.

The first of Carnevali's seven stages relates to the influences that will shape the nature of 'information acquisition, processing, and labelling' (Carnevali, 1983: 49). Pre-encounter influences include the diagnostician's professional education and clinical experience, not only in the particular area of nursing practice, but also in multicultural situations. Without educational preparation both in understanding the concept of culture as it relates to ethnic groups and in eliciting cultural information pertaining to client problems and situations (e.g. alcoholism, pregnancy), the nurse will have difficulty in ascertaining a client data-base that includes relevant, accurate and sufficient cultural information. Cultural cues will be missed, with consequent misdiagnosis.

Pre-encounter influences also include the environment in which the diagnostic encounter takes place. Schools, clinics, hospital wards and operating theatres are among the many environments in which nursing practice takes place. In each different environment, the nurse becomes accustomed to caring for certain types of clients (e.g. businessmen, disabled adolescents, pregnant women) presenting specific types of needs and concerns. There may be specific equipment and health promotional literature available appropriate to the usual range of clients and client problems that nurses encounter. The nurse becomes adept at noticing, recognizing and understanding certain problems more than

others, perhaps identifying child abuse in child health
clinics or diabetic crises in emergency departments. In
facilities serving many clients from a particular ethnic
group, nurses become adept at noticing pertinent cultural
cues and at reaching culturally appropriate diagnoses
relating to the specific ethnic group, especially if they have
been prepared educationally to understand how cultural
factors relate to client health.

If a British midwife or health visitor, for instance, were
geographically based, as s/he might be if part of a neighbourhood nursing service (DHSS, 1986), then, over a period of
time, s/he will have the opportunity to become well
acquainted with the cultural way of life and needs of
members of ethnic groups living in the locality. If s/he takes
this opportunity to become familiar with the culture of
ethnic groups in the neighbourhood, then as s/he interviews
a Greek Cypriot client, for example, s/he will be familiar
with Greek Cypriot culture, the varying kinds of cultural
concerns that may be raised and how cultural factors may
influence nursing care. Misdiagnosis due to lack of cultural
information is less likely to occur. By the same token, the
health visitor who works regularly with Vietnamese families, and who spends time becoming familiar with Vietnamese culture, will be less likely to diagnose child abuse in
instances when parents have availed their child of the
traditional Vietnamese lay therapy of *cao gio*, a form of
dermabrasion (Phillips, 1981).

The second stage of Carnevali's diagnostic process is
'entry into the data field'. This stage of the process requires
communication skills which promote 'efficient data sharing'
(Carnevali, 1983: 53), helping the client provide pertinent
information as efficiently and as comfortably as possible,
often within a limited time. People, however, vary as to the
ways in which they feel able to communicate with health
professionals. Sometimes a child will find it easier to
communicate through drawings (Parish, 1986), or perhaps
by play-acting with a doll or a puppet. Allowing the client to
present his/her concerns and needs in a manner in which
s/he feels comfortable, whether verbally, in drawing or in
play, is fundamental if the client is to provide insights into

his/her cultural values and way of life. At times, such as when interviewing the native Canadian Indian, an indirect approach to questioning may be more appropriate than the direct approach. The question: 'Where do you work?' might be phrased as 'Perhaps you have been working hard these days?', thereby saving the person who does not wish their identity to be exposed, from feeling embarrassed or discomforted (Hagey, 1986: 24).

Effective data-sharing involves encouraging the client to describe his/her concerns in cultural terms. Utilizing a health grid, Tripp-Reimer (1984; cf. Pearson and Vaughan, 1986: 42–3) highlights congruences and incongruences that may arise as to what health professionals and clients consider to be problematic or non-problematic regarding the client's health state. What is considered problematic in one culture may indeed be construed as non-problematic from a biomedical perspective, client and nurse each seeing the presenting situation or problem very differently, and each reaching conclusions grounded in differing perspectives.

While there may be 'no objective pathology that can be identified by a scientifically trained observer' (Tripp-Reimer, 1984: 106), the client may consider him/herself to be ill, perhaps suffering from a folk illness. One such folk illness is the 'evil eye'. Among the Greeks, this is known as *matiasma* which has its own 'elaborate preventive, symptomatic, diagnostic, and treatment practices', these being 'entirely outside the domain of biomedicine' (ibid). The nurse who is aware of Greek folk illnesses will be alert to the possibility of *matiasma*, and not be constricted to thinking only in biomedical terms.

The information a nurse requires to reach a culturally accurate nursing diagnosis may be wide-ranging. The nurse, for example, may need information about notions of cultural pollution, which in some cultures may relate to certain parts of the body being considered more unclean than other parts and/or to life events such as childbirth or menstruation (Sutherland, 1975; Homans, 1982; Ballard, n.d. [1983]). Information may also be needed about culturally-defined dietary beliefs and practices, such as the 'hot–cold' dietary belief system which is based on symbolic values associated with

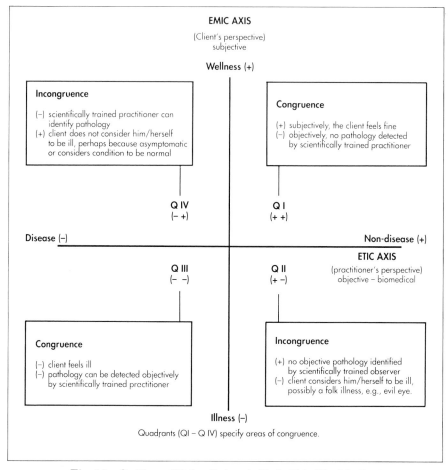

EMIC AXIS

(Client's perspective)
subjective

Wellness (+)

Incongruence

(−) scientifically trained practitioner can
identify pathology
(+) client does not consider him/herself
to be ill, perhaps because asymptomatic
or considers condition to be normal

Congruence

(+) subjectively, the client feels fine
(−) objectively, no pathology detected
by scientifically trained practitioner

Q IV
(− +)

Q I
(+ +)

Disease (−)   Non-disease (+)

ETIC AXIS

Q III
(− −)

Q II
(+ −)

(practitioner's perspective)
objective − biomedical

Congruence

(−) client feels ill
(−) pathology can be detected objectively
by scientifically trained practitioner

Incongruence

(+) no objective pathology identified
by scientifically trained observer
(−) client considers him/herself to be ill,
possibly a folk illness, e.g., evil eye.

Illness (−)

Quadrants (QI − Q IV) specify areas of congruence.

Fig. 16   Outline of Tripp-Reimer's Emic-Etic Health Grid

differing foods and foodstuffs and not temperature (Helman, 1985: 26–8). At times it may be important to know what cultural beliefs the client holds regarding his/her 'inner geography and functioning' (Kitzinger, 1972: 12), while in some situations, information may be required that relates to child socialization. Among the Inuit, playfulness is seen as important in child socialization (Briggs, 1979) and young children are seldom smacked, while in several European countries, such as Finland and Austria, there has been such concern about the number of children being hit or slapped that legislation has been passed to curb it (Potrykus, 1989). Various physical factors may also be culturally related, such as the consistency of cerumen which varies among racial/cultural groups (Matsunaga, 1962) and the presentation of cyanosis which differs with skin colouring, many cultural groups having a dominant skin colouring (Roach, 1977).

Gradually or swiftly, the nurse sorts out the relevant from the irrelevant cues, and coalesces them into patterns of recognition and organization. Carnevali describes this stage as 'developing cue clusters'. Throughout this stage, the nurse keeps an open mind, continually reviewing other ways in which data may be interpreted and whether or not the data-base is adequate. S/he considers different diagnostic possibilities, deciding whether the profile of one particular diagnosis fits the data better than another diagnostic profile. Does s/he require more information? What is the most likely diagnosis, and is it based on sufficient and accurate cultural information? What does the client and the client's significant others think? Eventually, the nurse decides on a particular diagnosis (or diagnoses). S/he considers that 'this' and not 'that' is what troubles or concerns the client, or, alternatively, describes some aspect of client wellness, and assigns an appropriate diagnostic label. But does the client have other ideas as to what is the diagnosis (or diagnoses), and, if so, on what is the client's diagnosis based? Has another health worker, perhaps a traditional healer (see e.g. Nemec, 1980; Assaad and El Katsha, 1981), already been consulted and what was this person's diagnosis? Is the nurse's understanding of the problem or situation adequate, and is s/he able to provide the form of help or guidance the client requires?

Planning, Implementation and Evaluation

While forming a diagnosis, or diagnoses, the nurse aims, as best s/he can, to gain insight into the client's cultural value system, information that will help him/her more ably to recommend and provide nursing care that will be acceptable to the client's way of life. Cultural values may be defined as enduring beliefs. They are abstract ideals which are accepted, implicitly or explicitly, by members of a particular cultural group, subsequently becoming determinants of the group members' behaviour (Rokeach, 1973; Bock, 1974; also Dobson, 1986). They govern how a client prioritizes health problems and how he, she or it (perhaps a family) deals with them. Advice that requires a client to contravene his/her cultural values is likely to be ignored, and, moreover, may result in the client preferring to cope as best s/he can, rather than follow advice that is culturally alien and so unacceptable.

There are now an increasing number of texts, journal articles, films and other sources of information to help nurses plan and implement nursing care along culturally sensitive lines (e.g. Leininger, 1984a; Mares, Henley and Baxter, 1985; Karseras and Hopkins, 1987; Boyle and Andrews, 1989b). In her text, *Community Culture, and Care*, Brownlee (1978) provides numerous reasons why it is important to ascertain certain items of cultural information. Why, for instance, is it important to know that a client, perhaps a Bangladeshi Muslim client, is keeping Ramadan (a time of fasting during daylight hours for members of the Islamic faith)? Does fasting during daylight hours affect whether or not the client can take medications or avail him/herself of immunization (Brownlee, 1978: 163)? In addition to guidance in the literature, there are usually formal or informal leaders among ethnic majority and minority groups who will gladly provide assistance and guidance to nurses unfamiliar with a particular culture or uncertain as to how to handle a specific cultural concern.

As the nurse moves on to the planning, implementation and evaluation stages of the nursing process, three concepts may be considered pivotal in intercultural situations, these are: caring, collaboration and creativity. The discovery of relevant cultural information in the assessment stage is but the prelude to the planning and delivery of sensitive and conscientious client care.

1. *Caring* implies a mental assent to the fact that both the action (e.g. some aspect of nursing care) and the recipient

of care are important to the caregiver (Kitson, 1985: 15). While caring includes discovering whether a pregnant Chinese mother plans to uphold culturally-defined post-partum traditions (see Pillsbury, 1978), it also involves hospital nurses as well as community nurses being careful to avoid recommending activities or foods that are culturally unacceptable postnatally. Caring may also mean making it possible for an elderly, hospitalized English woman to be visited by her cat or dog if this is her wish, or learning how to care for the Afro hairstyle of a West Indian patient (CRE, 1976). Caring involves making people feel cared for as cultural beings, and that their cultural values and traditions will be respected and, moreover, taken into account in nursing care.

2. *Collaboration* involves client and nurse working together, sharing ideas and doubts in the planning stages, as well as difficulties, successes and failures in the implementation and evaluation stages. It involves client and nurse finding new and creative ways to overcome obstacles that might impede the achievement of intended goals. It also involves 'participatory evaluation' (Feuer-stein, 1982) which emphasizes the shared nature of evaluation, Feuerstein describing this as it relates to the promotion of health at community level. Does the client consider s/he has been helped? What is still needing to be dealt with?

3. *Creativity* is an important attribute for nurses who work transculturally, yet is one that Jones (1983) considers to be poorly developed among many nurses. Where cultural perspectives of nurse and client differ considerably, much ingenuity may be needed if the client's cultural traditions are to be taken into account and blended skilfully into nursing care; for example, in finding interesting and meaningful ways in which a mentally disturbed client can develop a sense of self-esteem within culturally accept-able contours (Makar, 1970). Collaborating with the client as an equal, demonstrating in words, actions and sometimes silence a warm sense of caring, and being creative and imaginative in finding ways to interweave culture and care, are part and parcel of skilful transcul-

tural nursing, using the nursing process as an orderly and shared approach to care.

Obviously, it is much easier for nurses to provide culturally appropriate care when those who administer health care facilities and organizations not only permit, but indeed encourage, the integration of the client's cultural traditions within a Western scientific (or other, as applicable) medical setting. If the administrative staff are prepared to make long-term as well as short-term adjustments and adaptations to the facility and/or to the organization which will assist in the delivery of culturally sensitive health care, then clients will feel more at ease and less culturally alienated. 'Bringing the bush to the ward' in the form of 'branches from a red gum tree' tied to the intravenous posts of a hospital bed is an example of a short-term adaptation to a ward environment, one that helped ease the tremendous yearning for home felt by a hospitalized Australian Aboriginal woman (Crabbe, 1989: 17). An example of a long-term adaptation is in Arizona, where a hospital serving Navaho Indians has its entrance designed like a *hogan*, 'the traditional six-sided Navaho home, which has a doorway that always faces east' (Wagner, 1988: 24). At the far end of this facility, there is a room 'reserved for the performance of healing ceremonies, conducted by tribal medicine men. The room also is shaped like a *hogan* and features a wood stove in the middle' (ibid.). In both instances, positive attempts have been made to reduce the client's sense of cultural alienation in a Western scientific medical facility.

CULTURAL ASSESSMENT GUIDES

By and large, nurses care for clients whose problems and needs relate to life events, life crises and the client's place on the lifespan, and thus to times in people's lives such as the menarche, acute renal failure, bereavement and old age. Whether relating to lifespan, life events or life crises, the aim of transcultural nursing is to provide nursing care that is as congruent as possible with the client's cultural values, norms and practices as these relate to such times in the client's life. Whether nurses practise midwifery, occupational health nursing, oncological nursing, health visiting, long-term care of the elderly or are in one of the many other areas of nursing practice, they need to identify the client's cultural values, beliefs and practices as these influence and relate to the client's health problem and to the particular setting (e.g. hospital, home) (Tripp-Reimer, Brink and Saunders, 1984: 79).

There are now several cultural assessment guides available to help nurses discover pertinent cultural information in their everyday practice. These guides provide nurses with ideas that they might use to learn about the client and the client's situation in cultural terms when making client assessments. Not all clients will be prepared to share insights into their cultural ways, and here racial factors and other differences between client and practitioner may intrude (Sue, 1981: 63; Mares, Henley and Baxter, 1985). Cultural assessment guides should therefore be seen as guides to thinking, questioning and understanding which should be used thoughtfully and caringly. Some clients may need reassurance that in sharing cultural information, the nurse can, and will, use this information to provide care that will be more relevant and meaningful to the client.

While some guides focus on specific areas of nursing, such as Hilger's (1966) guide, which is concerned with maternal and child health, others are more comprehensive. A useful overview of cultural assessment guides is offered by Tripp-Reimer, Brink and Saunders (1984: 80), nine recognized guides being considered as they relate to four dominant focal areas (values, beliefs, customs and social structure components). Guides reviewed by Tripp-Reimer et al. (1984) include those by Branch and Paxton (1976), Brownlee (1978), Aamodt (1978) and Orque (1983).

One of the most comprehensive assessment guides is Brownlee's (1978) 'cross-cultural guide for health workers' which is geared primarily towards community assessment, and considered well suited as a guide to planning nurse education curricula (Tripp-Reimer et al., 1984: 79). Replete with a wide variety of ideas to consider, and utilizing a very understandable 'What–Why–How' approach to gathering information, Brownlee's text covers the following topics:

General community information;
Communication;
Language;
The family;
Politics;
Economics;
Education;
Religion;
Health beliefs and practices;
Traditional and modern health systems.

Nurses may turn to whatever section of Brownlee's text is relevant to their practice area and will find numerous ideas as to questions they might ask. If questions are phrased such that they are appropriate to the specific focus of nursing concern and to the client's situation and circumstance, these ideas may be used as a basis for interviewing the individual client as well as gathering information about the composite client (family, community or other social groups). Questions relating to what referral systems exist in the locality for people to use when they become ill, injured or pregnant (Brownlee, 1978: 219) can be posed at a community level, but they can also be rephrased to discover what alternative health care workers a client knows and, perhaps, uses or would use. The appendix in Brownlee's (1978: 285-7) text provides a useful checklist of general cultural patterns: 'forms of activity', 'forms of social relations', 'perceptions of the world' and 'perceptions of the self and the individual'.

Another assessment guide is Leininger's (1988: 157) diagrammatic 'Sunrise' model which includes the following seven components:

Technological factors;
Religious and philosophical factors;
Kinship and social factors;
Cultural values and lifeways;
Political and legal factors;
Economic factors;
Educational factors.

Depicted as set within an arch representing the cultural and social structure dimensions and world-view of a given culture, these seven components, which span out into a semi-

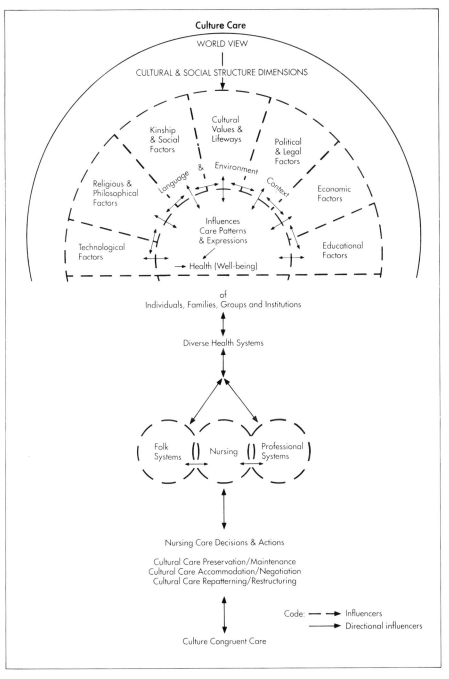

Fig. 17 Leininger's Sunrise model

circle (or 'Sunrise'), are seen as influencing care patterns and expressions through language and environment (Leininger, 1988: 157; also 1985a: 210), and are thus of importance to nursing care decisions and actions. Particular emphasis is given to three kinds of culturally-based nursing care decisions and actions: cultural care preservation (or maintenance), accommodation (or negotiation) and repatterning (or restructuring).

Focusing on the literature pertaining to depression, Rosenbaum (1989) indicates how various segments of Leininger's 'Sunrise' have relevance in intercultural situations to nurses caring for the depressed client. Political and legal factors, for instance, may influence the incidence of depression, there being a high incidence of depression among many refugees (Rack, 1982). Although some cultures do not have a linguistic and conceptual equivalence for the term 'depression', feelings of distress would appear to have a degree of universality, every language granting its members 'eloquence when it is time to cry for help', and every culture 'a rich set of idioms for the expression of distress aimed at mobilizing an effective social response' (Kirmayer, 1984: 159). The idea of both diversity and universality existing between cultures worldwide is basic to Leininger's (1988) theoretical framework. The 'Sunrise' model provides a gestalt view of the theory's major and interrelated components.

A third assessment guide, Orque's (1983: 10, 37) 'ethnic/ cultural system framework', incorporates yet another range of cultural components or elements:

Religion;
Art and history;
Value orientations;
Social groups' interactive patterns;
Language and communication process;
Healing beliefs and practices;
Family life processes;
Diet.

These are depicted as segments of a wheel, the hub of which represents basic human needs whose solutions 'lead to these

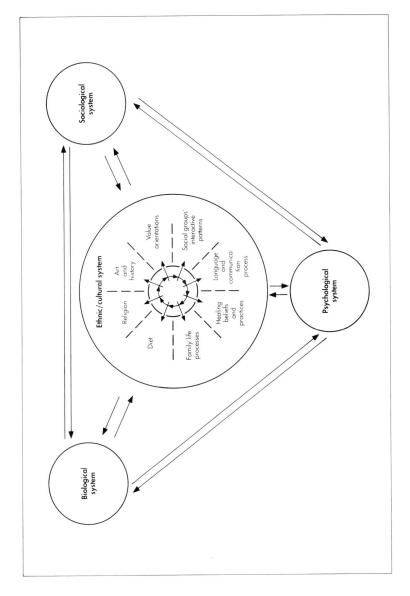

Fig. 18   Orque's ethnic/cultural system framework

cultural elements' (ibid.: 10). The wheel may be further envisaged as set within a triangle with its apices located in three interconnecting systems: biological, sociological and psychological. Although the various components of Orque's guide may be considered universal, each individual client is considered to have a unique cultural profile. No one member of a cultural group has the same life experiences nor has inherited their culture within the selfsame dimensions as another member of that same culture.

More recently, Herberg (1989: 24–5), in the text *Transcultural Concepts in Nursing Care* (Boyle and Andrews, 1989b), presents 'a guide for the assessment of cultural manifestations'. This is made up of eight main components:

Brief history of the origins of the cultural group, including location;
Value orientations;
Interpersonal relationships;
Communication;
Religion and magic;
Social systems;
Diet and food habits;
Health and illness belief systems.

Herberg emphasizes the need to understand the client's world-view, which she defines as the 'set of metaphorical explanations used' by a person of a given culture 'to explain life's events and offer solutions to life's mysteries' (ibid.: 21).

Tripp-Reimer (1984), who discusses cultural assessment from a 'values–beliefs–customs' stance, highlights the importance of nurses discovering how clients perceive and interpret their health state. The client's explanatory model, that is the beliefs and ideas that the client draws upon and uses to explain his/her particular problem or illness, is discussed at length by Kleinman (1980: 104–18; also Helman, 1985: 72–3) who provides the following series of questions which may be adjusted so that they are applicable to nursing situations:

1. What do you call your problem? What name does it have?
2. What do you think has caused your problem?
3. Why do you think it started when it did?

4. What does your sickness do to you? How does it work?
5. How severe is it? Will it have a short or long course?
6. What do you fear most about your sickness?
7. What are the chief problems your sickness has caused for you?
8. What kind of treatment do you think you should receive? What are the most important results you hope to receive from the treatment?
   (Kleinman, 1980: 106)

Another series of questions – in fact several question-naires – that have relevance to different areas of nursing practice and which seek to understand the client's cultural frame of reference, are presented by Helman (1985: 194–201; see also Littlewood, 1989: 227). Each of Helman's ten 'clinical questionnaires' relates to a separate chapter in his book *Culture, Health and Illness – an introduction for health professionals*, and concerns the following topics:

Cultural definitions of anatomy and physiology;
Diet and nutrition;
Caring and curing;
Doctor–patient interactions;
Pain and culture;
Culture and pharmacology;
Ritual and the management of misfortune;
Transcultural psychiatry;
Cultural aspects of stress;
Cultural factors in epidemiology.

Although cultural assessment guides/models vary as to focus and comprehensiveness, their purpose is to help nurses and other health workers to direct their thinking and questioning along clearly defined lines. As cognitive maps, they aim to direct the user's attention to aspects 'that will provide the most information relevant to the purpose of the observation' (Visintainer, 1986: 33). For the nurse, this would be to discover cultural information regarding the health of clients and patients as this relates to the practice of nursing. By the inclusion of what is deemed to be relevant to the purpose, maps thereby exclude what the map-maker considers irrelevant or less relevant. The effectiveness of maps hinges on 'their ability to abstract accurately the essential aspects of the territory' (ibid.: 35) under consideration. Although cultural assessment guides may be viewed as cognitive maps for use in field practice, some relating to specific 'terrains' (e.g. child health nursing), their usefulness depends on the nurse's ability either to select a guide that is appropriate to the client's particular situation or concern, or to use a comprehensive guide selectively.

Not only do individuals never learn their culture in its entirety – only the contours as these relate to the life he or she leads (Orque, 1983: 12) – but people differ as to how they interpret their culture in their own individual life situation. Hence, nurses need to be proficient in discovering cultural information for themselves, drawing upon information available in the literature, yet being independent of standard descriptions in order to avoid stereotyping. But if nurses are to glean skilfully, and with ease, cultural information pertinent to their clients' health needs and concerns, they must be given the opportunity to develop abilities in cultural discovery as part of their professional education.

ETHNOGRAPHY – AN APPROACH TO CULTURAL DISCOVERY

To be armed with a cultural assessment guide does not mean a nurse feels confident in using it. So how does the nurse become adept at cultural discovery? A sound beginning is clearly to have a genuine desire to learn about another culture. Although learning about another culture may seem like a limitless enterprise, in the reality of nursing practice it is shaped by the client's needs and concerns. Depending on the situation, different questions will be relevant. In some situations, how suicide is viewed by members of a given culture will be important, while in other situations whether pregnancies out of wedlock are considered acceptable or whether the elderly are accorded respect and, if so, how this respect is demonstrated may be relevant. Sometimes what seems to be a radical change in traditional values and normative behaviour may be but a minor modification. For

example, if an Inuit living in contemporary Canada considers using a residential home for elderly relatives, does
this constitute a radical break from tradition or a modification? (Older people traditionally lived with younger family
members in Inuit society.)

One fundamental requirement for providing culturally
appropriate care is to determine the client's ethnic identity,
that is, the ethnic group with which the client identifies.
Some people may have a very mixed ethnic background and
have little sense of identification with any one ethnic group,
while other people readily identify with a specific ethnic
group, perceiving themselves as belonging to a group of
people who have a common descent, a shared and inter-
generationally transmitted culture and a sense of group
consciousness (Smooha, 1985). An ethnic group, according
to De Vos (1975: 9), is a 'self-perceived group of people who
hold in common a set of traditions' (such as language and
religious beliefs) not shared by 'others with whom they are
in contact'. Although, for some people, national identity and
ethnic identity are one and the same, the term 'nationality'
usually embraces 'diverse groups that have achieved political unification' (De Vos, 1975: 11).

Ethnic identity is one form of client identification which
nurses do not always document, a major deterrent being the
possibility of information pertaining to the client's ethnic
group, especially if a minority group, being employed to the
group's detriment at a future point in time (cf. exclusion of
questions regarding ethnic information in national censuses: Bulmer, 1980). Yet it is both the client's and the
nurse's ethnic identity that conjointly determines whether
nurse–client encounters are inter- or intracultural and
whether transcultural nursing expertise is required (see
Dobson, 1988: 172). The basic intent in nurses knowing a
client's ethnic identity is that they will be able to offer
culturally appropriate nursing care which, because of its
cultural appropriateness, will both prove to be more effective and provide greater client satisfaction.

Two well-recognized qualitative research methods, ethnographic interviewing and participant-observation, have
potential as ways in which nurses might gain cultural

insight and understanding. Both methods are central to ethnographic fieldwork undertaken by anthropologists and sociologists, and are described in numerous publications written by anthropologists, sociologists and nurses (e.g. Byerly, 1976; Spradley, 1980; Hammersley and Atkinson, 1983; Ellen, 1984). But what is ethnography and how might it be adapted for use in nurse education and/or in everyday nursing practice? As a term, 'ethnography' is used both for the activity of learning about a culture in 'the field' and for the final description. As a research approach, which traditionally involves long-term immersion in one cultural group, ethnography involves systematically discovering and describing the regularities and variations of human social life with the purpose of understanding the structure and organizational principles of a specific cultural group. Spradley (1979: 3) emphasizes that ethnography means 'learning from people' who 'see, hear, speak, think, and act in ways that are different', that is culturally different from our own ways. For the nurse, 'ethnography is a means of gaining access to the health beliefs and practices of a culture' (Field and Morse, 1985: 21).

By observing, participating and interviewing, the ethnographer's aim is slowly to draw closer to understanding the 'social fabric' of a particular culture as lived by a certain group of people. What may seem inconsequential, the mere minutiae of life such as making a cup of tea for a guest, often reflects, in microcosm, the basic structure and values of the overall culture. Discovering the rules that are part of a culture and the regularities that shape it lies at the heart of ethnography. What customs are specific to the culture in question, how do they link together, and what values subsume them? What are the principles that guide members of this culture to act in certain ways and not in others, to make one decision rather than another? How would a person feel if certain cultural traditions were not upheld, and would this apply in all or only certain situations? How is health and illness defined, and what do people do to keep or become well?

For the nurse, or student nurse, gaining experience in cultural discovery might take the form of a mini- or attenuated ethnography, perhaps with a specific focus on one aspect of clinical nursing practice, and involving a small number of clients from one ethnic group (Dobson, 1986). This might be undertaken by one nurse or as a group enterprise. While it is envisaged that experience gained in this way would initially be within the parameters of an educational project (whether at basic or continuing educational level), the intent would be to provide each nurse with the opportunity to develop skills and abilities needed for cultural discovery in everyday nursing practice.

Sohier's (1978) account of nursing a Belgian Jew for an extended period of time until his death is an example of how, through observing, questioning and participating in the everyday life of members of a particular culture, a nurse can become increasingly able to provide culturally sensitive care. However, without the ease of access to the client's world and home circumstance that the community-based nurse has, yet also needing to deliver culturally sensitive and relevant care (Germain, 1982; Laughlin, 1989), the hospital-based nurse may find that gleaning cultural information requires continued vigilance and the use of every available opportunity. Opportunities within the context of hospital nursing practice might include the nurse enquiring about family and kinship relationships and responsibilities while bed-bathing a patient (and thus informally interviewing), observing family interaction during hospital visiting hours, and later becoming a participant in a family discussion relating to the patient's progress, noting which family member makes decisions on health and other issues (see Byerly, 1976).

Spradley and McCurdy (1972: 3) identify four steps which may need to be taken by such a project:

1. Understanding the culture concept and learning some field work methods.
2. Selecting a cultural scene and making contact with informants (e.g. clients).
3. Gathering and recording cultural data.
4. Analyzing the data and writing a cultural description.

Although the nurse is not engaged in formal research and

the methodological rigour attached to such endeavours, a mini- (or attenuated) ethnography would nevertheless be undertaken in the spirit of serious, though joyful, enquiry. It would be a planned opportunity for the nurse to gain in-depth understanding of a culture, with a view to planning, implementing and evaluating client-oriented nursing inter-ventions that are both efficacious and culturally mean-ingful. Such a project would clearly need to be undertaken with the clients' permission and, as applicable, that of the health organization/s providing client care.

Let us now consider briefly ethnographic interviewing, participation and observation, bearing in mind that in reality all three activities frequently overlap.

Ethnographic Interviewing

Ethnographic interviewing is directed specifically towards understanding the culture of a given group of people. As in all client interviews, warmth and sincerity should be con-veyed if the nurse wishes the client to divulge cultural information relating to his/her personal life or to the ethnic group to which he or she belongs. Tao-Kim-Hai's (1965: 150) description of his experience in a North American hospital highlights how impersonal health professionals, in this instance an anaesthetist, can be when interviewing. Tao-Kim-Hai describes questions as following one after the other without the slightest interrogative inflection in the anaes-thetist's voice: 'You have tuberculosis. You have venereal disease. You have . . .' When he asked the anaesthetist if he spoke French, the questioning resumed in the same manner: 'Vous avez la tuberculose. Vous avez des maladies vénér-iennes. Vous avez. . .' Information on interviewing tech-niques relevant to ethnographic fieldwork, including pit-falls to avoid and alternative ways to approach sensitive topics, can be found in many publications, some of which relate specifically to nursing (e.g. Payne, 1951; Schatzman and Strauss, 1973; Spradley, 1979; Leininger, 1984b; Field and Morse, 1985).

A notebook, a pen and, perhaps, a tape-recorder are the

basic tools the nurse needs when interviewing. It is important, however, that the client's consent for their use is
gained beforehand. It is also important that clients are
aware as to how the information they provide will be used
and assured that they may withdraw their consent at any
time. The nurse (or nurses, if a group project) keeps brief
notes relating not only to the interview itself (non-verbal as
well as verbal communication), but to the context in which
the interview is taking place. The nurse also includes his/her
own on-going ideas and thoughts, indicating these as such.
Should a tape-recorder be used, then interviews require
transcription. While time-consuming to transcribe, taped
interviews provide a chance to listen again to each word and
to the tenor of the conversation. Notes require expansion,
and preferably later that same day. Other data-collection
tools may also be used, such as ecomaps and genograms (see
Chapter 5) that highlight cultural information and, for
certain cultural groups, include appropriate anthropological symbols and format for kinship relationships (Dobson,
1989). Maps may be useful, perhaps to depict the location of
different health care facilities in relation to where families
and individuals interviewed live. How far do the clients have
to travel to the nearest hospital? Are they close to a
convenient bus route? Maps are a way of giving visual
impact to this type of information.

Once notes have been expanded and/or tapes transcribed,
the information is then divided into small chunks of information pertaining to differing themes so that they can later be
juggled about, clustered and re-clustered in differing ways
(Lofland and Lofland, 1984). In most instances, the nurse will
accrue a considerable amount of information needing to be
sifted through and analyzed. Information that initially has
fitted into one of the categories included in one or another
cultural assessment guide (e.g. hygienic practices as part of
'health beliefs and practices': Brownlee, 1978: 178–9) may
also become eligible for inclusion in a category that has
emerged from the interviews themselves, perhaps phrases
that clients have used regularly (e.g. 'coping with arthritis'),
such themes lending themselves to further exploration as
time permits. Guidelines as to how ethnographic and other

qualitative data may be analyzed are to be found in various publications pertaining to the research process (e.g. Field and Morse, 1985).

Participation and Observation

As described by Robertson and Boyle (1984: 45), partici-pation

> involves attendance at cultural functions, interactions with persons being observed, observation of activities, and, in some instances, direct participation in events and on-going life patterns.

Observation activities, however, 'concentrate on beha-viours as well as on the settings and circumstances in which behaviours are seen' (Robertson and Boyle, 1984: 45). As with interviewing, the nurse keeps notes about events and activities in which s/he participates and scenes and happen-ings that s/he observes. Although health professionals are usually keen observers, nurses should be careful to make observations that are directed towards patterns of beha-viour amongst members of the group being observed and not only individual behaviour (Peacock, 1986: 43).

Most cultural groups have specific places where members congregate from time to time, be it a club for members of a specific ethnic group (e.g. Polish clubs in Britain) or a building for religious worship where services are conducted in an ethnic minority language (e.g. Ukrainian churches in Canada). If the nurse wishes to learn about the Sikh religion, as s/he might if visiting Punjabi Sikh families, then s/he may wish to approach a family about the possibility of attending one of the services held at the Sikh temple (*gurdwara*). If invited, s/he may also be asked to partake in the *langar*, the community meal served after the service to the congregation in the community dining room. In attending both service and *langar*, the nurse will have gained much insight into the practice of Sikhism at that particular *gurdwara*.

Most nurses are well accustomed to observing and partici-pating in numerous 'events' which may range from a midwife participating in the delivery of an infant in a maternity hospital to a health visitor during a home visit observing a

Fig. 19   Example of a Ukrainian church near Batoche, Saskatchewan

child, just home from school, recounting the day's events to his mother. As well as providing new ideas and insights, observations allow nurses to check out and develop ideas they have gained previously, whether through interviewing, from earlier observations, or perhaps from the literature. How, for instance, does a *Bhatra* (a sub-caste: see Chapter 5) Sikh wife, for whom veiling before certain male members of the family is required, cope in a general public setting in the United Kingdom with the unexpected arrival of one of the menfolk in front of whom she should veil? The nurse can be watchful for ways *Bhatra* women use to achieve the intent of this custom when veiling might appear culturally alien in a public setting. The very fact that one such custom is modified, as it is in public settings, but nevertheless maintained (Dobson, 1987: 310–12), speaks volumes as to the importance of the cultural values that underpin this custom. What other customs are modified by other British Punjabi Sikhs and indeed by members of other ethnic minority groups, in order to appear acceptable in public settings where dominant cultural ways hold sway, such as in most hospitals, while maintaining conventional cultural behaviour when among members of their own cultural group (e.g. Anwar, 1979: 222)?

Religious artifacts can be especially important items for nurses to observe. When visiting *Bhatra* Sikh homes, a health visitor might notice that a picture of *Sher-vali* ('she who belongs to the tiger') is to be seen in several homes (Dobson, 1987: 309), and will discover that *Sher-vali* is a goddess of the Hindu pantheon considered powerfully able to help women who long to conceive a child, and particularly a son. Although members of the Sikh faith hold to the words of the Sikh Gurus, on further questioning the health visitor will discover that, in the Indian Subcontinent, a respected holy person or being of another religion, if deemed powerful, may be approached should the need arise. The need to bear a son to perpetuate the lineage is especially important to Indian families.

The use of rooms in a home and typical arrangement of domestic furniture is culturally defined, and is information that may be useful to many community nurses. Among the Sikh families that the author visited in the United Kingdom (Dobson, 1987, e.g. 281–3), it was usual for the front room or parlour (the *betak*) to be used by the men for entertaining their male friends and other important guests. The rooms the women regularly used were towards the back of the home, a reflection of the patriarchal nature of Punjabi society. Thresholds are also important points to notice, and may be either real ones such as doorways in a client's home, or symbolic ones such as the entrance to a new stage of life (e.g. marriage, birth). The lintel of the outside door to a Punjabi Sikh home and of several doors inside the home (such as the one where a newborn baby boy is being kept) are decorated with the *schree* (bundles of leaves, which in the United Kingdom may be from the *Acuba japonica*), which indicates that a baby boy has been born and helps to protect the room/ house (and thus the baby) from harmful and malevolent forces. Certain people who have power to control access to important commodities, such as money, access to health care and leisure time, may also be viewed as symbolic thresholds. It is important for nurses to know who is the 'gatekeeper' to certain health decisions and actions in a given cultural group, if the nurse is to use culturally correct channels for promoting health in a family or community.

Photography

Bit by bit, the nurse builds up a profile of the cultural group in relation to the specific clinical nursing focus chosen. With the permission of the client/s and, as applicable, of those who administer the health facility, the nurse might wish to take photographs – perhaps of ways in which children are typically handled and cared for by members of the cultural group, or perhaps of traditional healing rituals or ways of preparing foods (see Mead and Macgregor, 1978). Photographs of general scenes can also be useful, providing an opportunity to look again at selected scenes, and to look for details missed while observing other aspects of the cultural scene, details which may help to generate new ideas or illuminate others (Collier, 1967; Crane and Angrosino, 1974: 157–76). In addition, photographs may be used within a mini- or attenuated ethnography to illustrate cultural themes such as thresholds or perhaps colours which carry symbolic power (see Birren, 1978) and have possible relevance for health promotional materials such as posters. With video-recorders becoming increasingly commonplace in today's society, their use (with accompanying annotations) might also be considered within quite a small-scale project.

Concerns Relating to Self

Certain factors may intrude upon a nurse's ability to notice and interpret cultural cues, ethnocentricity being one such impediment, while other factors, such as gender and parenthood, may influence whether or not a client relates easily to a nurse from a different cultural group.

Ethnocentricity
Each one of us is ethnocentric; that is, bound by a specific cultural outlook set within a certain period in history. Collecting information relating to a culture other than our

own requires recognition of our own ethnocentric bias, and a willingness and an ability to emancipate ourselves, in some measure, from our own cultural view, becoming more 'perceptive, sensitive, and receptive' (Leininger, 1984b: 113) to the other person's or group's cultural values and ways of living.

For the most part, it is the stranger who sees 'the taken-for-granted nature of culture' (Burtonwood 1984: 278), aspects that we hardly notice about our own culture which stand out more starkly to someone from another culture. Viewing our culture as an 'outsider' looking in is often difficult (Kleinman, 1980: 26), and it is usually easier, at least initially, to learn about a culture dissimilar to one's own. However, as we learn to comprehend another culture, our own cultural traditions and values are often thrown into sharp relief, and traditions and values, which perhaps we had never questioned before, beg to be understood.

Being a nurse
Having been socialized professionally into certain ways of acting and reacting, nurses may find it difficult to step back and look at their work and their clients with 'new eyes'. On the other hand, it is the very fact that they are nurses that allows them to feel comfortable within a nursing situation and to know what has relevance to nursing practice (Pearsall, 1965: 38). One aspect of a nurse's professional socialization is learning to value certain standards of hygiene. As a consequence, a nurse's reaction to an unkempt, 'dirty house' (Lentz and Meyer, 1979) may be exceptionally biased and rigid, and distract him/her from being alert to the client's abilities, perhaps those of being a loving and tolerant parent. Ethnographic observations should be as free as possible from the nurse's own cultural and professional biases, the overall aim being to find ways in which care might be made more culturally sensitive, relevant and efficacious for the client.

But how might the client's perception of nurses and nursing affect the type and amount of information the client provides? Fagin and Diers (1984) suggest that metaphorical underpinnings of nursing include motherhood, intimacy and sex. Does the nurse's gender, for example, affect the type of information she or he will glean about a client's culture (Easterday et al., 1982; Ardener, 1984)? Will a male health visitor be able to interview Punjabi women about pregnancy and parturition? Two male researchers who studied social and religious features of a Punjabi Sikh community in Wales 'never saw a glimpse of a woman' (Thomas and Ghuman, 1976: 29), while another researcher, Dosanjh (1976: 91), who looked at Punjabi and English childrearing practices in England, conducted very few interviews with Punjabi mothers (often their husbands were present) on his own, his wife or niece accompanying him on the majority of interviews. He comments that a female interviewer may be a 'more suitable person to interview Punjabi mothers' (Dosanjh, 1976: 91).

Far from being 'a faceless robot or a machinelike recorder of human events' (Powdermaker, 1967: 19), each nurse has a personality of his/her own. But to what extent does the nurse's personality, and also the nurse's age, influence his/her access to certain types of cultural information? How much difference does being married and/or being a parent make to the information clients will offer? While undertaking anthropological fieldwork on lay health ideology and health behaviour in south India, Nichter and Nichter (1987) found that being parents with a young child made them much more eligible to become privy to a wealth of cultural information on local childcare and childrearing practices than when they were childless. While the answers to these questions will vary from culture to culture, they nevertheless need consideration before, during and after any ethnographic project which involves discovering the client's world through face-to-face encounters.

CONCLUSION

In this final section the focus has been on the need for nurses to gain experience in developing proficiency in cultural discovery, and the idea of using ethnographic methods in a mini- or attenuated form has been put forward as a possible approach to achieving this. Other qualitative methods may also be used, such as a life history of one client (Leininger, 1985b; King, 1989), or the use of ethnoscience, a linguistically-based approach to cultural discovery which focuses on how people construe their world and make sense of their everyday life from the way they talk about it (Evaneshko and Kay, 1982; Morse, 1983). Learning about cultural groups and their ways as these apply to nursing care is an activity in which all nurses should be involved to some extent as part of their basic and continuing professional education. To know more about other people's cultures and to gain a greater understanding of one's own cultural ways calls for a special enthusiasm from nurses who are keen to give their clients the very best of care.

REFERENCES

Nursing Process

Aggleton P and Chalmers H (1986) *Nursing Models and the Nursing Process*. Basingstoke: Macmillan.

Allodi F, Berger P, Beyersbergen J and Fantini N (1986) Community consultation on refugee integration. Central American refugees and survivors of torture in Ontario. *Canada's Mental Health* **34**(4): 10–12.

Andrews MM (1989) Transcultural perspectives in the nursing care of children and adolescents. In JS Boyle and MM Andrews (eds) *Transcultural Concepts in Nursing Care*. Glenview, IL: Scott, Foresman.

Assaad M and El Katsha S (1981) Villagers' use of and participation in formal and informal health services in an Egyptian delta village. *Contact* [Bulletin of the Christian Medical Commission, Geneva], No. 65: 1–13.

Ballard R (n.d. [1983]) *The Implications of Cultural Diversity for Medical Practice. An anthropological perspective*. Unpublished manuscript. Applied Anthropology Group, University of Leeds.

Bock PK (1974) *Modern Cultural Anthropology. An introduction*, 2nd edn. New York: Knopf.

Boyle JS and Andrews MM (1989a) Transcultural perspectives in the nursing process. In JS Boyle and MM Andrews (eds), *Transcultural Concepts in Nursing Care*, Glenview, IL: Scott, Foresman.

Boyle JS and Andrews MM (eds) (1989b) *Transcultural Concepts in Nursing Care*. Glenview, IL: Scott, Foresman.

Briggs JL (1979) *Aspects of Inuit Value Socialization*. National Museum of Man, Canadian Ethnology Service, Paper No. 56. Ottawa: National Museums of Canada.

Brink PJ and Saunders JM (1976) Cultural shock. Theoretical and applied. In PJ Brink (ed.), *Transcultural Nursing. A Book of Readings*, Englewood Cliffs, NJ: Prentice Hall.

Brown Y, Calder B and Rae D (1989) Female circumcision. *The Canadian Nurse* **85**(4): 19–20, 22.

Brownlee AT (1978) *Community, Culture and Care. A cross-cultural guide for health workers*. St Louis, MO: CV Mosby.

Cardenas B and Lucarz J (1985) Canadian Indian health care. A model for service. In M Stewart, J Innes, S Searl and C Smillie (eds), *Community Health Nursing in Canada*. Toronto: Gage.

Carnevali DL (1983) *Nursing Care Planning: Diagnosis and management*, 3rd edn. Philadelphia: Lippincott.

Carnevali DL (1984) The diagnostic reasoning process. In DL Carnevali, PH Mitchell, NF Woods and CA Tanner (eds), *Diagnostic Reasoning in Nursing*. Philadelphia: Lippincott.

Crabbe G (1989) Healing the dreamers. *Nursing Times* **85**(13): 16–17.

CRE (Commission for Racial Equality) (1976) *Afro Hair, Skin Care and Recipes*, 3rd edn. London: CRE.

Davitz LL and Davitz JR (1985) Culture and nurses' inferences of suffering. In LA Copp (ed.), *Recent Advances in Nursing*, [Perspectives on pain.] **11**.

DHSS (Department of Health and Social Security) (1986) *Neighbourhood Nursing. A focus for care. Report of the Community Nursing Review*. London: HMSO.

Dobson S (1986) Cultural value awareness. Glimpses into a Punjabi mother's world. *Health Visitor* **59**(12): 382–4.

Dobson SM (1988) Diagnosis and the health visitor. *Senior Nurse* **8**(4): 15–17.

Dobson SM (1989) Conceptualizing for transcultural health visiting. The concept of transcultural reciprocity. *Journal of Advanced Nursing* **14:** 97–102.

Feuerstein MT (1982) Participatory evaluation. By, with and for the people. *Idea* [RRDC Bulletin], March: 18–23.

Fuller JHS and Toon PD (1988) *Medical Practice in a Multicultural Society*. Oxford: Heinemann.

Gregory DM (1988) Nursing practice in native communities. In AJ Baumgart and J Larsen (eds), *Canadian Nursing Faces the Future. Development and change*. St Louis: CV Mosby.

Griffith-Kenney JW and Christensen PJ (eds) (1986) *Application of Theories, Frameworks, and Models*, 2nd edn. St Louis: CV Mosby.

Hagey R (1986) Anishnawbe health resources and the indirect approach. *Nutrition Newsletter* [Health and Welfare Canada], No. 7: 23–5.

Hagey RS and McDonough P (1984) The problem of professional labelling. *Nursing Outlook* **32**(3): 151–7.

Hall ET and Whyte WF (1960) Intercultural communication. A guide to men of action. *Human Organization* **19**(1): 5–12.

Helman C (1985) *Culture, Health and Illness. An introduction for health professionals*. Bristol: Wright.

Hofstede G (1980) *Culture's Consequences. International differences in work-related values*. Beverly Hills, CA: Sage.

Homans H (1982) Pregnancy and birth as rites of passage for two groups of women in Britain. In CP MacCormack (ed.), *Ethnography of Fertility and Birth*, London: Academic Press.

Hostetler JA and Huntington GE (1970) The Hutterites. Fieldwork in a North American communal society. In GD Spindler (ed.), *Being an Anthropologist*. Prospect Heights, IL: Waveland Press.

Houldin AD, Saltstein SW and Ganley KM (1987) *Nursing Diagnoses for Wellness. Supporting strengths*. Philadelphia: Lippincott.

Jansen G (1973) *The Doctor–Patient Relationship in an African Tribal Society*. Assen, The Netherlands: Van Gorcum.

Jenny JL (1987) Knowledge deficit. Not a nursing diagnosis. *Image* **19**(4): 184–5.

Jones JA (1983) Where angels fear to tread. Nursing and the concept of creativity. *Journal of Advanced Nursing* **8**: 405–11.

Karseras P and Hopkins E (1987) *British Asians. Health in the community*. Chichester: John Wiley.

Kim MJ, McFarland GK and McLane AM (eds) (1989) *Pocket Guide to Nursing Diagnoses*, 3rd edn. St Louis: CV Mosby.

King LS (1967) What is a diagnosis? *Journal of the American Medical Association* **202**(8): 154–7.

Kitson A (1985) Educating for quality. *Senior Nurse* **3**(4): 11–13, 15–16.

Kitzinger S (1972) Body fantasies. *New Society* **21**(510): 12–13.

LaFargue JP (1980) A survival strategy. Kinship networks. *American Journal of Nursing* **80**(9): 1636–40.

Leininger MM (1984a) *Reference Sources for Transcultural Health and Nursing*. Thorofare: Slack.

Littlewood J (1989) A model for nursing using anthropological literature. *International Journal of Nursing Studies* **26**(3): 221–9.

Makar DH (1970) Communication through the language barrier. *Nursing Times* **66**: 971–2.

Mares P, Henley A and Baxter C (1985) *Health Care in Multiracial Britain*. Cambridge: Health Education Council/National Extension College.

Martin J and Walsh K (1981) Another world. *Nursing Times – Community Outlook*, 12 March: 96–7, 99–100.

Matsunaga E (1962) The dimorphism in human normal cerumen. *Annals of Human Genetics* **25**: 273–86.

Mitchell GJ and Santopinto M (1988) An alternative to nursing diagnosis. *The Canadian Nurse* **84**(10): 25–8.

Nemec J (1980) Rediscovering an ancient resource. A new look at traditional medicine. *Contact* [Bulletin of the Christian Medical Commission, Geneva], No. 58: 1–18.

Orque MS, Bloch B and Monrroy LSA (eds) (1983) *Ethnic Nursing Care. A multicultural approach*. St Louis: CV Mosby.

Parish L (1986) Communicating with hospitalized children. *The Canadian Nurse* **82**(1): 21–4.

Pearson A and Vaughan B (1986) *Nursing Models for Practice*. London: Heinemann.

Phillips S (1981) Bizarre physical signs and traditional Vietnamese folk medicine. *Maternal and Child Health* **6**(4): 145–7.

Pillsbury BL (1978) 'Doing the month'. Confinement and convalescence of Chinese women after childbirth. *Social Science and Medicine* **12**: 11–22.

Potrykus C (1989) Hitting children is wrong. *Health Visitor* **62**(6): 169.

Potter PA and Perry AG (1987) Cultural factors in health. In *Basic Nursing. Theory and practice*. St Louis: CV Mosby.

Qureshi B (1986) Dealing with patients from different cultures. *Midwife, Health Visitor and Community Nurse* **22**(12): 436, 438, 447.

Rhodes H (1980) Ismail's world. *Nursing Times – Community Outlook*, 8 May: 139–40, 145, 147, 150.

Roach LB (1977) Assessment. Color changes in dark skin. *Nursing '77* **7**(1): 48–51.

Rokeach M (1973) *The Nature of Human Values*. New York: Free Press.

Roper N, Logan WW and Tierney AJ (1990) *The Elements of Nursing: A Model for Nursing based on a Model of Living*. 3rd edn. Edinburgh: Churchill Livingstone.

Spradley BW (1981a) The helping relationship and contracting. In *Community Health Nursing. Concepts and practice*, 1st edn. Boston, MA: Little, Brown.

Spradley BW (1981b) The nursing process in community health. In *Community Health Nursing. Concepts and practice*, 1st edn. Boston, MA: Little, Brown.

Sutherland A (1975) *Gypsies. The hidden Americans*. London: Tavistock.

Tann SP and Wheeler EF (1980) Food intakes and growth of young Chinese children in London. *Community Medicine* 2(1): 20–4.

Tripp-Reimer T (1984) Reconceptualizing the construct of health. Integrating emic and etic perspectives. *Research in Nursing and Health* 7(2): 101–9.

Wagner L (1988) Blending old traditions with modern medicine. *Modern Health Care* 18(35): 22–8.

Wright AF (1953) The Chinese language and foreign ideas. In AF Wright (ed.), *Studies in Chinese Thought*, 55(5) Part 2, Memoir No. 75. Menasha, WI: American Anthropological Association.

Yura H and Walsh MB (1988) *The Nursing Process*, 5th edn. Norwalk, CT: Appleton & Lange.

Cultural Assessment Guides

Aamodt AM (1978) Culture. In AL Clark (ed.), *Culture, Childbearing, Health Professionals*, Philadelphia: Davis.

Boyle JS and Andrews MM (eds) (1989b) *Transcultural Concepts in Nursing Care*. Glenview, IL: Scott, Foresman.

Branch MF and Paxton PP (eds) (1976) *Providing Safe Nursing Care for Ethnic People of Color*. New York: Appleton-Century-Crofts.

Brownlee AT (1978) *Community, Culture, and Care. A cross-cultural guide for health workers*. St Louis: CV Mosby.

Helman C (1985) *Culture, Health and Illness. An introduction for health professionals*. Bristol: Wright.

Herberg P (1989) Theoretical foundations of transcultural nursing. In JS Boyle and MM Andrews (eds), *Transcultural Concepts in Nursing Care*, Glenview, IL: Scott, Foresman.

Hilger MI (1966) *Field Guide to the Ethnological Study of Child*

Life. Behavior Science Field Guides. **1,** 2nd edn. New Haven, CT: Human Relations Area Files Press.

Kirmayer LJ (1984) Culture, affect and somatization. *Transcultural Psychiatric Research Review* **21:** 159–88.

Kleinman A (1980) *Patients and Healers in the Context of Culture*. Berkeley, CA: University of California Press.

Leininger MM (1985a) Transcultural care diversity and universality. A theory of nursing. *Nursing and Health Care* **6**(4): 208–12.

Leininger MM (1988) Leininger's theory of nursing. Cultural care diversity and universality. *Nursing Science Quarterly* **1**(4): 152–60.

Littlewood J (1989) A model for nursing using anthropological literature. *International Journal of Nursing Studies* **26**(3): 221–9.

Mares P, Henley A and Baxter C (1985) *Health Care in Multiracial Britain*. Cambridge: Health Education Council/National Extension College.

Orque MS (1983) Orque's ethnic/cultural system. A framework for ethnic nursing care. In MS Orque, B Bloch and LSA Monrroy (eds), *Ethnic Nursing Care. A multicultural approach*, St Louis: CV Mosby.

Rack PH (1982) Migration and mental illness. A review of recent research in Britain. *Transcultural Psychiatric Research Review*, **19**(3): 151–72.

Rosenbaum JN (1989) Depression: viewed from a transcultural nursing theoretical perspective. *Journal of Advanced Nursing*, **14**(1): 7–12.

Sue DW (1981) *Counselling the Culturally Different. Theory and Practice*. New York: John Wiley.

Tripp-Reimer T (1984) Cultural assessment. In JP Bellack and PA Bamford (eds), *Nursing Assessment. A multidimensional approach*. Monterey, CA: Wadsworth.

Tripp-Reimer T, Brink PJ and Saunders JM (1984) Cultural assessment. Content and process. *Nursing Outlook* **32**(2): 78–82.

Visintainer MA (1986) The nature of knowledge and theory in nursing. *Image* **18**(2): 32–8.

Ethnography – an Approach to Cultural Discovery

Anwar M (1979) *The Myth of Return. Pakistanis in Britain*. London: Heinemann.

Ardener S (1984) Gender orientations in fieldwork. In RF Ellen (ed.), *Ethnographic Research. A guide to general conduct*. London: Academic Press.

Birren F (1978) *Color and Human Response.* New York: Van Nostrand Reinhold.

Brownlee AT (1978) *Community, Culture, and Care. A cross-cultural guide for health workers.* St Louis: CV Mosby.

Bulmer M (1980) On the feasibility of identifying 'race' and 'ethnicity' in censuses and surveys. *New Community* 8(1–2): 3–16.

Burtonwood N (1984) Multicultural education. Education for a multicultural society or multicultural individuals? *New Community* 11(3): 278–9.

Byerly EL (1976) The nurse-researcher as participant-observer in a nursing setting. In PA Brink (ed.), *Transcultural Nursing. A book of readings.* Englewood-Cliffs, NJ: Prentice Hall.

Collier J (1967) *Visual Anthropology. Photography as a research method.* New York: Holt, Rinehart & Winston.

Crane JG and Angrosino MV (1974) *Field Projects in Anthropology.* Morristown, NJ: General Learning Press.

De Vos G (1975) Ethnic pluralism. Conflict and accommodation. In G De Vos and L Romanucci-Ross (eds), *Ethnic Identity. Cultural continuities and change.* Palo Alto, CA: Mayfield.

Dobson S (1986) Ethnography. A tool for learning. *Nurse Education Today* 6: 76–9.

Dobson SM (1987) *The Role of the Health Visitor in Multicultural Situations.* Unpublished PhD thesis. University of Edinburgh.

Dobson SM (1988) Ethnic identity. A basis for care. *Midwife, Health Visitor, and Community Nurse* 24(5): 172, 176, 178.

Dobson SM (1989) Genograms and ecomaps. *Nursing Times,* 85(51): 54–6.

Dosanjh JS (1976) *A Comparative Study of Punjabi and English Child Rearing Practices with Special Reference to Lower Juniors (7–9 years).* Unpublished PhD thesis, University of Nottingham.

Easterday L, Papademas D, Schorr L and Valentine C (1982) The making of a female researcher. Role problems in fieldwork. In RG Burgess (ed.), *Field Research. A sourcebook and field manual.* London: Allen & Unwin.

Ellen RF (ed.) (1984) *Ethnographic Research. A guide to general conduct.* London: Academic Press.

Evaneshko V and Kay MA (1982) The ethnoscience research technique. *Western Journal of Nursing Research* 4(1): 49–64.

Fagin C and Diers D (1984) Nursing as a metaphor. *International Nursing Review* 31(1): 16–17.

Field PA and Morse JM (1985) *Nursing Research. The application of qualitative approaches.* London: Croom Helm.

Germain CP (1982) Cultural concepts in critical care. *Critical Care Quarterly* **5**(3): 61–78.

Hammersley M and Atkinson P (1983) *Ethnography. Principles in practice.* London: Tavistock.

King PA (1989) A woman of the land. *Image* **21**(1): 19–22.

Kleinman A (1980) *Patients and Healers in the Context of Culture.* Berkeley, CA: University of California Press.

Laughlin A (1989) Smiles are all part of the treatment at the Children's. *The Gazette* [Montreal], 30 June: J1.

Leininger M (1984b) Transcultural interviewing and health assessment. In PB Pedersen, N Sartorius and AJ Marsella (eds), *Mental Health Services. The cross-cultural context,* Beverley Hills, CA: Sage.

Leininger MM (1985b) Life health-care history. Purposes, methods, and techniques. In MM Leininger (ed.), *Qualitative Research Methods in Nursing.* Orlando, FL: Grune & Stratton.

Lentz JR and Meyer EA (1979) The dirty house. *Nursing Outlook* **27**(9): 590–3.

Lofland J and Lofland LH (1984) *Analyzing Social Settings. A guide to qualitative observation and analysis,* 2nd edn. Belmont, CA: Wadsworth.

Mead M and Macgregor FC (1978) Growth and culture. A photographic study of Balinese childhood. In T Polhemus (ed.), *Social Aspects of the Human Body,* Harmondsworth: Penguin Books.

Morse JM (1983) An ethnoscientific analysis of comfort. A preliminary investigation. *Nursing Papers* **15**(1): 6–19.

Nichter M and Nichter M (1987) A tale of Simeon. Reflections on raising a child while conducting fieldwork in rural South India. In J Cassell (ed.), *Children in the Field.* Philadelphia: Temple University Press.

Payne SL (1951) *The Art of Asking Questions.* Princeton, NJ: Princeton University Press.

Peacock JL (1986) *The Anthropological Lens. Harsh light, soft focus.* Cambridge: Cambridge University Press.

Pearsall M (1965) Participant observation as role and method in behavioral research. *Nursing Research* **14**(1): 37–42.

Powdermaker H (1967) *Stranger and Friend. The way of an anthropologist.* London: Secker & Warburg.

Robertson MH and Boyle JS (1984) Ethnography. Contributions to nursing research. *Journal of Advanced Nursing,* **9**(1): 43–9.

Schatzman L and Strauss AL (1973) *Field Research. Strategies for a natural sociology.* Englewood Cliffs, NJ: Prentice Hall.

Smooha S (1985) Ethnic groups. In A Kuper and J Kuper (eds), *The Social Science Encyclopedia*, London: Routledge & Kegan Paul.

Sohier R (1978) Gaining awareness of cultural difference. A case example. In M Leininger (ed.), *Transcultural Nursing. Concepts, theories, and practices*, New York: John Wiley.

Spradley JP (1979) *The Ethnographic Interview*. New York: Holt, Rinehart & Winston.

Spradley JP (1980) *Participant Observation*. New York: Holt, Rinehart & Winston.

Spradley JP and McCurdy DW (1972) *The Cultural Experience. Ethnography in complex society*. Chicago: Science Research Associates.

Tao-Kim-Hai AM (1965) Orientals are stoic. In JK Skipper and RC Leonard (eds), *Social Interaction and Patient Care*. Philadelphia: Lippincott.

Thomas DA and Ghuman PA (1976) *A Survey of Social and Religious Attitudes among Sikhs in Cardiff*. Cardiff: The Open University in Wales.

Transcultural Nursing

Health Visiting in the UK

In this final chapter, the initial focus is on the provision of transcultural community health nursing in a multicultural society, more specifically transcultural health visiting in the United Kingdom. For those unfamiliar with British health visiting, a short description of its history and intent is provided. Thereafter, findings are presented from a study of twenty-nine Punjabi families in the United Kingdom, an exploratory study which considers various aspects of childbearing and childrearing relevant to the practice of health visiting. With interviews paralleling in various ways conventional health visiting in nature, content and timing, it is suggested that this study helps demonstrate that information about clients' cultural traditions and background, and relevant to health visiting, can be uncovered by health visitors in everyday practice, given that they have received educational preparation in cultural discovery. As pre-encounter influences, these findings may be considered to be part of a health visitor's 'cerebral library', cultural information that s/he draws upon when caring for a Punjabi family from a similar community. The final focus of this chapter is on transcultural nursing in more general terms.

In many parts of the globe, nurses care for multicultural clienteles and need to be skilful in transcultural nursing care. Like British health visitors, they require the support and input that nurse educators, administrators and researchers can provide towards the encouragement and development of transcultural nursing. Indeed, if nurses,

British health visitors included, are to provide transcultural
nursing care, sensitively blending culture and care along
client-centred lines, then they need the opportunity to
become educationally prepared in the discovery and utiliza-
tion of cultural information. They also require an organizational milieu in which transcultural nursing care is both
encouraged and facilitated. With many nurses working as
part of interdisciplinary teams of health professionals, the
provision of transcultural care often assumes dimensions
wider than nursing itself, the need for culturally relevant,
client-oriented approaches to health care becoming a concern that nurses share with other health professionals.

COMMUNITY   HEALTH   NURSING – HEALTH VISITING

Community health nursing services have been formed in
response to perceived needs in different countries at different times in history. In New Zealand, the Plunket Society
(named after Lord Plunket, then Governor-General of New
Zealand, and his wife) was formed in 1907 to provide parents
with advice and assistance free of cost so that mothers and
their offspring would be rendered more 'hardy, healthy, and
resistive to disease' (Rattray, 1961: 71). Almost two centuries
earlier, the order of the Sisters of Charity of Montreal, better
known as the Grey Nuns or *Soeurs Grises*, were pioneers in
community nursing from the 1730s onwards, providing care
for early settlers in Canada and for native peoples (Gibbon,
1947: 46, 85–90).

In the United Kingdom, the health visiting service
emerged in response to the needs of the urban poor during
the industrial revolution of the nineteenth century when
dramatic increases in urban living were paralleled by
concomitant increases in the density of poverty, disease and
squalor. During the second half of the nineteenth century,
various voluntary groups were formed to help alleviate
human misery and ill-health, one such group being the
Ladies Sanitary Reform Association. Formed in Manchester
and Salford in 1862, this association is considered to be the

direct antecedent of today's health visiting service. By 1899, the infant mortality rate in England and Wales was standing at 163/1000 (McCleary, 1935: 4–5), and the need to improve maternal and child health had become a national concern, one which led to the development of the infant welfare movement. While the idea of a nationwide service began to take shape during the early years of the twentieth century, the provision of a health visiting service did not become a statutory requirement of local authorities until the passing of the National Health Service Act in 1946 (United Kingdom, 1946).

Today, health visiting is an unsolicited, universalist and nationwide public service, which utilizes home visiting as its dominant approach to client care. As defined by the Council for the Education and Training of Health Visitors (CETHV, 1977: 8), 'the professional practice of health visiting consists of planned activities aimed at the promotion of health and prevention of ill-health'. Concerned with 'teaching the principles of healthy living', health visitors help families and individuals from all walks of life to build up their 'personal resources so that they can better cope with the normal crises of life' (RCN, 1971: 9). Nationally funded and bureaucratically organized, health visiting has evolved into a statutory service with its own professional education and a code of conduct. With its clientele drawn from contemporary Britain's multicultural/multiracial society, the service continues to be community-based and health promotional in orientation, caring for clients from various cultural traditions.

Although differing conceptual frameworks may be used by health visitors to guide their practice in various client situations (see Orr, 1985: 92–3; McClymont, Thomas and Denham, 1986: 330–42), it is vital that the client's 'customs, values and spiritual beliefs' (UKCC, 1984: 2) are taken into account if health visiting practice is to be relevant to the client's needs in the context of the client's culture. With the aim of helping the client achieve and maintain an optimal level of health, the practice of health visiting is intended to be a participative process undertaken: 'within the framework of the personal philosophy and cultural value systems of the client, and with self-determination accorded [to] the client, as far as is compatible with the rights and needs of others' (CETHV, 1977: 30–1).

MATERNAL AND CHILD HEALTH VISITING – CARING FOR PUNJABI FAMILIES

Health Visiting's Maternal and Child Health Remit

Although contemporary health visitors care for a variety of client groups, they are still most readily identified with their maternal and child health remit, a remit which involves the provision of on-going care for both the pregnant mother and the under five-year-old population. Pregnancy is one time when the health visiting service focuses on the health and well-being of the woman. The mother has become the human environment in which a member of a future generation is growing. Depending on her/his caseload, and giving priority to the first-time mother, the health visitor makes an assessment of potential and actual problems relating to both the mother's and the unborn baby's health and well-being. By visiting antenatally, s/he provides the mother, and her family, with an opportunity to talk at some length, and in the privacy of the home, about socio-emotional as well as physical problems, whether on-going or foreseen. For the married pregnant woman, problems may relate to wifehood as well as to motherhood, and the health visitor must visualize his/her client as both wife and expectant mother. By listening, counselling and advising as appropriate, the health visitor aims to help the mother remain well throughout her pregnancy and to promote as secure and loving a home environment as possible for the newborn baby.

Until the tenth day postpartum, the mother and infant are visited by the midwife. During this time, the midwife supports the mother as she recuperates from the experience of childbirth and adjusts to caring for her newborn infant in addition to her other family responsibilities. Thereafter, the health visitor begins visiting the family on a long-term basis, developing a health visitor–client relationship within which the health and well-being of each family member can be promoted. During each visit, the health visitor determines whether the family has any health problems or concerns for which s/he can provide help and guidance of either a direct or an anticipatory nature.

A Study of Punjabi Families Using Ethnographic Approaches

Let us now consider the provision of culturally sensitive health visiting to a Punjabi family with at least one child under five years old, drawing on findings from an exploratory study which focused on childbearing and childrearing practices among twenty-nine Punjabi families with at least one child under five years old and residing in an urban location in Britain (Dobson, 1987). It is suggested that the findings of this study, which were gleaned through the use of ethnographic approaches to cultural discovery, are similar to those that a practising health visitor, visiting families from a similar Punjabi community, might elicit over a period of time, given that his/her workload was not unduly demanding and that s/he had received educational preparation in cultural discovery. Most of the interviews took place between 10 am and 5 pm, Monday to Friday, and thus were within conventional health visiting hours. Respondents were aware that the interviewer was a health visitor (although a non-practising one) and that the information they provided was to be directed towards increasing health visitors' understanding of the families' cultural traditions. Many of the visits were approximately one hour in duration, the length of time that a health visitor might spend when making an initial assessment visit to a client's home (and similar in duration to many of the visits made by health visitors in Clark's (1985: 100, 245) study of health visiting). As clients are usually aware of the serial nature of health visiting, it is likely that the mothers would have proffered as much (if not more, rather than less) cultural information to a practising health visitor who was directly involved in promoting the family's health as they would to a non-practising health visitor/researcher, as in the research study. It is recognized, however, that considerable time and energy is involved not only in the collection of cultural information, but also in the collation and analysis of information gleaned, time that might not be available to many practising health visitors.

In collecting this information, sixty-six visits were made to the twenty-nine families. Visits were also made to several Punjabi families with children over five years of age, to a number of Punjabi individuals, and to various organizations and people concerned with the care of South Asian families. Several services were attended at the local Sikh temple. Although the twenty-nine families were divided by religious affiliation (to Islam and Sikhism), and with the partition of the Indian Subcontinent in 1947 might be considered as being either of Pakistani or Indian background, a Punjabi culture pervaded and unified both groups (Dobson, 1987: 196). All families spoke Punjabi, nearly all the women interviewed wore Punjabi-style clothing (i.e. the *salwar-kameez*, a trousers and tunic outfit), both groups enjoyed a similar type of diet, and the joint family system was a guiding force if not a living reality. (The joint family, as upheld in the Indian Subcontinent, traditionally involves both the budget and the maintenance of the family property being of a joint nature with the eldest male maintaining authority, although a certain fluidity in the meaning of 'jointness' is accepted: Bell, 1968: 58; Anwar, 1979: 52–7.)

Of the twenty-nine families, twenty were of the Islamic faith and nine upheld Sikhism. As religion is a dominant force in Punjabi communities, some general information about the Islamic and Sikh faiths is in order (see e.g. Henley, 1982, 1983; Iqbal, 1981; Sampson, 1982). Unlike Islam, Sikhism originated in the Punjab itself, developing under the leadership of several Gurus, notably Guru Nanak who founded the religion in the late fifteenth century, and Guru Gobind Singh who challenged the faith of his followers in 1699 and instituted the five 'K's', or articles of faith, worn by Sikhs to this day. The five 'K's' are: a steel bangle worn on the right wrist (*kara*), unshorn hair (*kes*), a special comb worn in the hair (*khanga*), a pair of shorts (*kachha*) which may be worn as undergarments, and a type of sword (*kirpan*) or a miniature version of the same. Islam, which dates back to the seventh century AD, originated in Arabia and was brought to the Punjabi plains by traders and conquering armies, such as those of Mahmud of Ghazni (a town in Afghanistan) and of Timur (also known as Tamurlane). The doctrines of Islam, known collectively as the *Qur'ân*, are based on the words of Allah as revealed through the Archangel Gabriel to the Prophet Muhammad. The Islamic faith has five pillars: the proclamation of the faith, formalized prayers which are said facing towards the holy city of Mecca, almsgiving, fasting and the performance of pilgrimage (*hajj*) to the holy places of Islam, notably Mecca and Medina.

Without involving a sense of a hierarchy based on levels of purity, such as those on which the Hindu caste system is based, sub-caste membership still holds a position of some importance amongst British Punjabis, Muslims and Sikhs, both in the formation of social networks and in the arrangement of marriages (see Werbner, 1979: 27–8, 48–9). While very little information was collected during the study that related specifically to sub-castes among the Muslim families visited (e.g. the *Arain* sub-caste), information specific to the *Bhatra* sub-caste, to which the majority of Sikh families interviewed belonged, was collected. According to Hindbalraj Singh (1977: 10), the first group of *Bhatra* Sikhs arrived in Britain in 1924. Prior to partition of the Indian Subcontinent, many *Bhatra* families lived near Sialkot, a town north of Lahore, then in West Punjab and now in Pakistan. During partition, *Bhatra* families living in the Sialkot area fled to India to find new homes in and around cities such as Amritsar and Delhi. Some, with kinsmen in Britain, migrated to the United Kingdom.

All of the twenty-nine mothers interviewed were married and living with their husbands. Families lived in a variety of housing types in different parts of the city, though most of the Sikh families lived near the Sikh temple (*gurdwara*). The majority of mothers were conversationally fluent in English, and had a variety of British accents, reflecting the mobility of many Punjabis throughout the United Kingdom, whether for marital or economic reasons. In only five families was an interpreter needed, and then another adult or older adolescent member of the family obliged. Many of the families, especially among the Sikh community, had lived in the United Kingdom for some time, eight of the twenty Muslim mothers for over six years and eight of the nine Sikh mothers for between ten and twenty-nine years. Three of these eight Sikh mothers were born, raised and educated in the United Kingdom.

When interviewing the mothers, some of whom were visited more than once, an interview schedule was used to help focus conversations and facilitate the collection of personal base-line information, such as age and religious affiliation (Dobson, 1987: 198–9, 455–60). While lending a more formal air to an interview, an interview schedule can help provide the respondent with a clearer understanding of the focus of the study (Bott, 1957: 21). Questions in the schedule related to several topics, including previous pregnancies, infant feeding and sources of advice and influence regarding maternal and child health. Several questions required the recall of past decisions (e.g. the commencement of bottle-feeding) and events (e.g. pregnancies) (cf. Orr, 1980: 43). Although memory acts selectively and people have their own biases in the recollection of events (Moser and Kalton, 1971: 331; Atkinson, 1971: 80), 'the essence tends to be remembered' (Dosanjh, 1976: 105), even though exact details may be forgotten.

When considering the findings presented below, which provide insight and ideas for use by health visitors when visiting Punjabi families and individuals in the United Kingdom, it is important to bear in mind that these findings relate to one group of Punjabi families in one location during one particular period of time, and that emphasis has been given to the *Bhatra* Sikh families. Although the findings listed below are presented as relating to different 'clients' – the Punjabi woman as wife, the antenatal Punjabi mother, and the post-natal Punjabi mother and infant – there is a certain degree of overlap, some findings relating to more than one 'client'.

A. *Findings Relating to the Punjabi Woman as Wife*

1. The patriarchal, patrilocal and patrilineal nature of Punjabi society was evident among the families visited; that is, the men have authority, on marriage a woman moves to live in the husband's home and inheritance is through the male line. In several instances, couples lived in joint family households.

2. The pervasiveness of religious beliefs and practices. Not only was religious affiliation (whether to Islam or Sikhism) identifiable in practically every home by the display of religious artifacts, but religion provided a reason for the women to gather together, for instance to read the *Qur'ân* and for services at the Sikh temple (*gurdwara*).

3. The continuance of the joint family system. Where it was not feasible for family members to live in close proximity to each other (e.g. due to transglobal migration), links were maintained by other means, for example through intermittent visits, going on the *hajj* together, and requesting grandparents in the Subcontinent to name a newborn grandchild. Where the joint family household existed, the mother-in-law dominated the female hierarchy. However, in accord with the patriarchal nature of the Punjabi family system, senior women are subject to the traditional dominance of male family members.

4. The view of the *biraderi* (the brotherhood) as a cohesive and mutually supportive social network which also acts as a form of social control, and may follow sub-caste divisions (e.g. *Arain* Muslims). Among the *Bhatra* families, intra-*biraderi* cohesiveness was maintained in various ways, including emphasis on regular attendance at the *gurdwara*, and by upholding the custom of *vartan bhanji*, a reciprocal gift exchange system in which a degree of imbalance is maintained to indicate the intent to continue inter-family relationships (see Wakil, 1970: 702).

5. The maintenance of the custom of arranged marriages. The choice of bride for groom is a parental decision which may be made with the help of a match-making intermediary (*vichola*), 'someone who knows someone'

(Dobson, 1987: 298) and who acts as a go-between.

6. The assumption of junior status within the female hierarchy of the joint family household by the wife on marriage. The *Bhatras* are divided into clans, and further subdivided into lineages, each with their own code of lineage behaviour (Dobson, 1987: 292). For the newly-wed *Bhatra* wife, adjusting to the affinal family (her in-laws) includes learning a new code of lineage behaviour. While the traditional power of the senior members of the joint family is reduced in nuclear family households, it may continue indirectly.

7. The maintenance of honour (*izzat*). A *Bhatra* wife, for instance, upholds the *izzat* of her affinal family by maintaining sexual propriety as well as by showing respect for senior family members. This includes *Bhatra* wives veiling before their male affines (in-laws).

8. The relevance of religious affiliation to marriage customs. While divorce is acceptable but in no way desired by Muslim families, it is considered exceptional among the *Bhatra* Sikhs. While marriages of close relatives are preferred within the Muslim community, among the *Bhatra*, a woman should marry a husband outwith the clans of both her parents, although a son can marry into his mother's though never into his father's clan.

9. The importance amongst the *Bhatra* families of demonstrating fecundity early in marriage (cf. Homans, 1982: 235). Special emphasis is placed on bearing a son.

10. The maintenance of Punjabi cultural traditions. Adjustments may be made to certain traditions within non-Punjabi settings, facial veiling, for example, being omitted by *Bhatra* wives in public places other than at the *gurdwara*. In addition to those identified above, cultural traditions upheld included traditions relating to language, dress, dietary beliefs and code of hygiene, some of which are noted below.

B. *Findings Relating to the Antenatal Punjabi Mother*

1. The increase in status that pregnancy provides the wife within the affinal family. In one sense, the baby belongs to

the joint affinal family as a whole and not to the parents alone. For the *Bhatra* wife, male progeny provide her with greater status than do female progeny.

2. The importance of religio-cultural beliefs and practices to conception, particularly to bearing a son, and to the safeguarding of pregnancy. Traditional health practitioners (e.g. a *hakim*, a *baba* or a *devi*) and Western scientific health practitioners might be consulted for similar concerns. (A *hakim* is a physician who practises *Unani* medicine. A *baba* is a man of the Sikh faith who is considered to possess God-given powers of healing, and a *devi* is the female equivalent of a *baba*.)

   Bhatra wives anxious to bear a son will offer prayers to the Sikh Gurus, and also to *Sher-vali*, the goddess from the Hindu pantheon. Some wives will keep the fast of *Purnmashi* in the hope of being blessed with a son. Commencing on the birthday of Guru Nanak (the founder of the Sikh faith), this fast is kept on the day of the full moon of each lunar month, often for a whole year (Dobson, 1987: 309).

3. The acceptance of Western scientific health care with regard to pregnancy and confinement. Most Sikh mothers recalled attending for their initial antenatal examination during the first and second months of the first trimester of pregnancy, and earlier than the Muslim mothers remembered attending, especially in regard to second and subsequent pregnancies.

4. A view of pregnancy as a time of increased vulnerability to powerful forces which can both harm the unborn child and cause the pregnant mother to miscarry. A miscarriage is considered by *Bhatra* families to be much more polluting than childbirth (Dobson, 1987: 333; cf. Lozoff, Kamath and Feldman, 1975: 356). Culturally defined measures are used by members of the *Bhatra* community to counteract these forces. A *ruchya*, for instance, an amulet on a black thread received from a *baba* or *devi*, might be worn to help ensure that a pregnancy is carried to term.

5. The maintenance of an interrelated 'hot–cold' (*garam– thanda*) foods and bodily conditions belief system. *Bhatra*

families hold an all-female pregnancy party (*gon*) during the seventh (preferably) or ninth month of pregnancy when the pregnant mother is given *punjeeri*, a 'hot' (*garam*) food substance, by her guests. Being *garam*, *punjeeri* is not taken in any quantity, if at all, until the ninth month, as pregnancy is considered a 'hot' condition which must be kept in 'balance' (cf. Homans, 1983: 75; Nichter and Nichter, 1983: 240). Recipes for *punjeeri* (known by Muslim families as *dabra*) varied. Essentially, *punjeeri* is a food of a soft texture made of a variety of ingredients, often clarified butter (*ghee*), sugar, milled almonds, coconut, pistachio nuts, ginger and *chapatti* flour. Dietary cravings of pregnancy include those relating to Indo-Pakistani foods, such as tamarind (*imbeli*), chillis, mangoes and *pakoras* (a spicy food made out of pulse flour and fried in oil).

6. The minimal uptake of formal antenatal classes by pregnant mothers. This finding relates to towns and cities countrywide where twenty-six of the twenty-nine mothers had lived during their pregnancies in the United Kingdom (Dobson, 1987: 321–3; cf. Jones and Dougherty, 1982: 288).

C. *Findings Relating to the Post-natal Punjabi Mother and Infant*

1. The maintenance, when socially possible, of an approximately forty-day, customary post-natal period known as the *chalia* (or *sawa maheena*) when the mother is considered to be in a polluted condition, that is in cultural terms. For the *Bhatra* mother, this cultural pollution is reduced through a series of ritual baths taken at decreed times during the *chalia*. The infant also receives ritual baths at similar times. On the thirteenth or twenty-first day postpartum, depending on circumstances such as the mother's physical well-being, the ritual bath known as the *chaunka chalia* is taken, signifying that the mother is ritually clean enough to return to work in the house and kitchen. On the fortieth day, the *Bhatra* mother and infant take their final ritual baths and attend the *gurd-*

wara for the *mata takon* (bowing before the *Guru Granth Sahib* – the Sikh Scriptures) when they are reincorporated formally into the *Bhatra* community.

For the Muslim mother, the *sawa maheena* (literally 'one and a quarter months' and equivalent in intent to the *chalia*) is a time when the mother is forbidden to touch the *Qur'ân* (a form of ritual distancing), though she may listen to it being read. It is also a time when the mother is considered to be in a weaker condition and should avoid undue strain on her body, some mothers preferring not to read, sew or knit at this time (Dobson, 1987: 334).

2. The maintenance of culturally defined post-natal dietary beliefs. In particular, *garam* foods (e.g. *punjeeri*; *dahl* – split pea of the gram), nutritious liquids (e.g. chicken gravy, milk) and softened foods (e.g. rice or lentils blended into a watery consistency) were among those recommended.

3. The maintenance of religio-cultural ceremonies for infants. Among the Muslim families, the *azan* (the Muslim call to prayer) is recited into each ear of the newborn infant, and the infant's head tonsured and nails clipped in early infanthood. Circumcision is performed routinely on male Muslim infants/children. Many Sikh infants receive the initial letter for their name from a randomly opened page of the *Guru Granth Sahib* during the *mata takon*. A personal thanksgiving to *Sher-vali* might be made at this time.

4. The protection of *Bhatra* infants (especially male infants) from harmful forces through the maintenance of certain cultural practices. These include the maintenance of a strict *chalia* (the 40-day postpartum period) for the infant, placing a black mark on the infant's forehead to deflect evil forces, tying a black thread (*thaga*) on the infant's wrists, ankles and/or waist, and by hanging the *schree* (see Chapter 4) across a number of door lintels in the home.

5. The use of a vessel or jug (*lota*) for pouring water onto the perineum for cleansing purposes, for instance after defecation or vaginal loss. With the *lota* held in the right hand, which is considered ritually clean, water is poured

onto the perineum which is touched only by the unclean
left hand.
6. Although over half of the seventy-two infants born live to
the mothers interviewed were initially breast-fed, most
mothers remembered bottle-feeding infants raised in the
United Kingdom by eight weeks postpartum.

Transcultural Nursing: Health Visiting

Before looking at how some of the findings might be used in
relation to the health visitor's maternal and child health
remit, let us review the intent of transcultural nursing and,
in this instance, transcultural health visiting. The aim of
transcultural nursing is to provide care that is as congruent
as possible with the client's cultural values, norms and
practices. In addition to implying the presence and awareness of a cultural disparity between practitioner and client,
the term 'transcultural', as used by the author, denotes the
coexistence of an affirmative, conscious desire by the nurse,
and it is hoped also by the client, to bridge and transcend
cultural differences within the nurse–client relationship. It
implies a prescription for practice. Like transcontinental
and transoceanic journeys which conjure up a sense of
adventure and excitement as new vistas, lifestyles and a
kaleidoscope of new experiences beckon the would-be tra-
veller, transcultural nursing/health visiting takes on a
similar imagery with the prefix 'trans' encapsulating both a
sense of movement between client and nurse of ideas,
knowledge and respect, and the challenge of being culturally creative and innovative in nursing (Dobson, 1988a: 63).
Recognizing the limitations that ethnocentricity places on
his/her ability to practise effectively in intercultural situations, the practitioner strives to emancipate him/herself
from his/her own cultural view. The reciprocation of cultural knowledge and respect between practitioner and client
is considered integral to transcultural nursing and as
increasing in spiral fashion as the nurse–client relationship
becomes more collaborative in nature. Rather than only a
few nurses being proficient in transcultural nursing, it is
envisaged that all nurses working in multicultural societies

will receive educational preparation in transcultural nursing and become proficient in providing culturally sensitive care for multicultural clienteles.

Using Cultural Information

Viewed as pre-encounter influences (Carnevali, 1983), the above findings may be considered to be information that the health visitor has discovered previously and which s/he draws upon when caring for other Punjabi families with a child under five years old or for a pregnant Punjabi wife in a similar Punjabi community. While some findings clearly relate to Muslim Punjabis and others to Sikh Punjabis, findings relating to the uptake of antenatal classes (B6 above) and to bottle-feeding infants by eight weeks postpartum (C6 above) need to be explored further in relation to the wider population as well as in regard to Punjabi cultural traditions. Let us now look at how some of these findings might be used to provide culturally sensitive care for the pregnant wife and the recently delivered mother.

Visiting the Pregnant Punjabi Woman as Wife

When visiting the pregnant wife, the health visitor determines whether the mother-to-be is confident about the health and well-being of herself and her unborn infant, parturition and the postpartum period. The health visitor is also concerned about the stability of the marriage and any other concerns relating to wifehood which may lead to the baby being born into a stressful home situation. Is the wife experiencing 'emotional strain relating to wifehood', and, if so, does she feel she is coping effectively or not? To be able to help a Punjabi wife who is experiencing emotional strain of this nature, indeed perhaps severe marital discord, the health visitor must be able to perceive the wife's personal situation within the context of Punjabi culture (Dobson, 1989a). In any culture, factors relating to emotional strain of this type may include difficulties in adjusting to a new marriage, to a new locality on marriage, and to developing a new socio-emotional support system, as well as marital discord not related specifically to being newly wed. With a sound knowledge base of the concept of culture, the health visitor is better able to direct his/her data searches along pertinent, culture-specific lines, to make culturally relevant and astute diagnoses, and to plan interventions that have relevance to the context and circumstance of the wife's situation and the wife's cultural value system.

When arranging a marriage for their children, Punjabi families consider the compatibility of the two joint families to be vital, indeed an essential precondition to the overall happiness of the couple. For some health visitors, the collective intent of arranged marriages may be somewhat alien, Punjabi marriages being marital alliances, which link two joint families together, with love and companionship between groom and bride expected to develop after the wedding and not before, and frequently within the wider family setting. Arranged marriages, like most marriages, may or may not lead to sustained conjugal happiness. (One glowing affirmation spontaneously declared by one of the mothers in the study was that 'arranged marriages are lovely': Dobson, 1987: 298.) Where a love-match does not emerge, but instead a marriage with which the couple are mutually dissatisfied, then the custom of arranged marriages might be considered a factor predisposing to a situation of emotional strain.

Traditionally, a new bride begins married life in the joint family household. Where this occurs, she also assumes junior status within the female hierarchy, beginning married life under the domination of her mother-in-law. For the *Bhatra* wife, not only may her mother-in-law be someone she has scarcely known, if at all, until after the wedding, but early days of married life in a joint family household are a time when she needs to be as skilful as possible in managing several new human relationships at one time. As a junior member of this household, she must uphold the *izzat* of her natal family by coping with marital difficulties without complaint. The health visitor must therefore be sensitive to the possibility of a Punjabi wife hesitating to vocalize negative feelings lest, in so doing, this reflects adversely on the *izzat* of her natal family should members of her affinal family realize that she has voiced such dissatisfactions. While the Punjabi husband also has to uphold the *izzat* of his natal family, and is himself under the domination of the senior male family members, the restrictions placed on the Punjabi wife tend to be more constraining than those placed on the husband.

Although the wife who begins married life in a nuclear existence may not need to be as skilful at managing as many human relationships at one time as she would had she entered a joint family household, she may find it a very lonely existence if she has hitherto lived in a joint family household. Having known very little of each other prior to marriage, the newly wedded Punjabi couple living in a nuclear situation may have to make immense personal adjustments, although if sufficient wisdom and sensitivity have been accorded to spouse selection, such adjustments may be minimal.

While difficulty in adjusting to a new locality on marriage is in no way culture-specific, for the newly married Punjabi wife it may involve considerable adjustments. For the Punjabi woman who travels to Britain from the Subcontinent to be married or to join her husband, not only is the British landscape very different from the Punjabi one, but the secular nature of contemporary Britain contrasts markedly with the audio-visual pervasiveness of religious practices in everyday life in the Subcontinent (Dobson, 1985). Internal migration within Britain may also bring contingent strains and a sense of dislocation, for instance where a wife moves to a community that is much more orthodox than her natal community.

Should the wife find it difficult to make friends within her affinal family, and if she is having difficulty adjusting to the expectations and personality of her mother-in-law, then she may be in a particularly stressful situation. For the husband, friction between his wife and mother may place him in a very difficult position, given that senior members of Punjabi households should be accorded respect. Various opportunities exist for wives to make friendships outwith their affinal family. Muslim women, for instance, gather together to read the *Qur'ân* and for various Islamic celebrations such as *Eid-*

ul-fitr which marks the end of *Ramadan* (the month when Muslims fast from dawn to dusk), while Sikh wives meet other women at services held at the *gurdwara* and at special celebrations in the homes of other Sikh families. Friendships may also be made with people met in other settings, perhaps at child health clinics, or at the mother's workplace where this is applicable (very few of the women interviewed worked outside the home other than in businesses run by the family), or through various organizations linked to schools their children attend.

With emphasis placed on bearing a child early in marriage, especially a son who will help to perpetuate the lineage, a wife who is pregnant for the first time may still be adjusting to life in the affinal household and to a husband whom she scarcely knew before marriage. It is therefore important that the health visitor considers the various emotional strains relating to wifehood that a Punjabi wife pregnant for the first time may be experiencing. But it is not only the newly wedded wife who has problems of marital adjustment and concord. Marital discord and dissension may occur at various times in Punjabi marriages, as it does in marriages among members of other ethnic groups.

While desertion or divorce may be contemplated by a Punjabi couple, the possible consequences of these options may increase rather than lessen a wife's emotional strain if they are known to bring other culturally defined difficulties in their wake, for dissolution of marriage in Punjabi society, like its arrangement, extends beyond the couple themselves. While the possibility of divorce is unlikely among Sikh couples, it is accepted, but with reluctance, among Muslim couples for whom marriage is a civil institution rather than the sacred and indissoluble institution it is considered within Sikhism. While divorce is an alternative that an unhappy Punjabi wife might consider in the United Kingdom, it is one that, for the Sikh wife, will lower the *izzat* of her natal family, severely reducing her own remarriage prospects and making it more difficult thereafter for members of her natal family to find suitable marriage partners. Should the children of the marriage be seen as belonging to the joint family, then the wife, whether Muslim or Sikh, who contemplates divorce may also face social opposition from her husband's family should she seek custody of the children.

While information on spousal abuse was not elicited during the study (Dobson, 1987: 376), it does exist in Punjabi communities (Anonymous, 1980; 1986: personal communications) as it does among other ethnic groups (majority and minority) throughout the United Kingdom. By tradition, the *biraderi* endeavours to rectify serious instances of marital disharmony and division, and is a definite strength of Punjabi cultural life. However, many wives, both as married and unmarried women, will have been dependent on kin for support throughout most, if not all, of their lives. It can therefore be surmised that it would be both emotionally and financially difficult, at least initially, for a Punjabi wife to be a woman alone.

Counselling, the purpose of which is to assist clients in making their own decisions from the choices available to them, is a dominant mode of health visiting intervention relevant to helping a wife cope with emotional strain relating to wifehood. But, for a non-Punjabi health visitor to guide a Punjabi wife's thoughts and conversation along appropriate channels, cultural insight, sensitivity and understanding are essential, both in regard to the wife's individual circumstance and, where this applies, to the joint family situation. While an individualist approach may be suitable for a wife living in a nuclear existence, it may be neither suitable nor feasible for a wife living in a joint family household. Given the corporate nature of joint Punjabi families, a collectivist (a group-oriented) approach may be more suitable, the health visitor working with the extended family rather than with the wife or the nuclear couple alone. However, because of the sensitive nature of family *izzat* in Punjabi culture, the health visitor must first win the family's trust as someone actively interested in understanding the nuances of Punjabi family life and marriage customs and keen to provide guidance and support that is culturally relevant and acceptable.

If the wife is pregnant and/or has small children, the health visitor needs to ensure as best s/he can that a tense marital situation is eased, and endeavour to counsel in ways that are culturally acceptable to the client. At times, due to workload and other factors, it may be impossible for health visitors to offer in-depth counselling, and families with marital problems may need to be referred elsewhere for further help and support. In situations where a Punjabi community is small, families may have difficulty finding someone who understands sufficiently their cultural way of life to be able to provide culturally sensitive and relevant support. There are, however, many community-based organizations in cities and towns throughout the United Kingdom that are geared specifically towards helping ethnic minority families, including those with serious, on-going family and marital problems. But the service that they offer is distinctly different from that of health visiting and should not be seen as a substitute in a multicultural society for the provision of a multiculturally relevant health visiting service.

Health Visiting the Post-natal Punjabi Mother

When the health visitor makes his/her initial post-natal visit, s/he is concerned whether the mother has recovered adequately from the stress (physical and emotional) of childbirth, whether she and other family members are coping well with their newborn baby, and whether the baby is healthy and content. Traditionally, the young Punjabi mother is mentored in the art of mothercraft by a female relative, usually by her mother or mother-in-law (cf. Gideon, 1962). For the Punjabi mother who lives in a nuclear family household and is distant from her natal or affinal kin, the *puerperium* (the six to eight weeks following parturition when the mother physically and emotionally recuperates from childbirth) may be a time when she not only lacks this traditional mentorship but feels the rift from close kin with particular acuteness, adding thereby to her vulnerability to post-natal depression (Dobson, 1988b: 176).

As very few mothers from the predominantly secular majority culture of the United Kingdom continue to uphold religio-cultural post-natal practices, such as the ʿchurching of women' (Staton, 1981), many health visitors may fail to recognize the importance that religio-cultural practices have for the Punjabi mother. During the *chalia/sawa maheena*, which traditionally lasts for forty days or there-abouts, various religio-cultural practices are important to many Punjabi mothers, and need to be recognized as such by the family's health visitor. As well as being a time of celebration, the post-natal period is a time of cultural pollution and vulnerability for mother and infant. For the *Bhatra* family, the *schree*, the *thaga* and the black mark placed on the infant's forehead (or elsewhere on the face) are important for protecting the baby from evil or powerful forces, and must be respected by health visitors as being vital to the infant's well-being in cultural terms. For Muslim families, the tonsuring ceremony involves shaving off the hair on the baby's head, hair that has been polluted through the process of childbirth. Other practices, such as post-natal mothers taking ritual baths at certain times or ritually distancing themselves from the *Qur'ân*, reflect a Punjabi view of the post-natal mother as in a state of cultural pollution. For the *Bhatra* mother, this state of cultural pollution is reduced with each ritual bath and is formally ended when she attends the *gurdwara* for the *mata takon*. Should the help of *Sher-vali* have been sought antenatally, then thanks are also offered to her at this time.

Showing an interest in these and other traditional post-natal practices, allowing for them and including them whenever possible when giving advice (e.g. regarding baby bathing, and perhaps recommending that the *chaunka chalia* be postponed when a mother has had a Caesarian section) is fundamental to the formation of culturally accurate diagnoses, to the provision of culturally sensitive care and to the development of health visitor–client relationships based on cultural respect and knowledge.

As cultural practices may vary in some measure from community to community, health visitors need to know what is right and correct for the Punjabi mother to do according to traditional ways upheld in the client's community. Does the mother, for example, view her physical condition (i.e. the post-natal state) within the 'hot–cold' belief system, and, if so, what kind of advice is considered appropriate? Is the mother using the 'hot–cold' dietary belief system in her choice of food and liquid refreshment at this time? Although recommended as putting 'strength' into the post-natal mother (Dobson, 1987: 326; also Homans, 1983: 76), *punjeeri/dabra* is considered by some mothers as being 'too greasy' or too fattening (Dobson, 1987: 327). With a good knowledge of Punjabi dietary practices, the health visitor is better informed to suggest alterations or additions to the mother's diet that align Punjabi dietary norms with Western dietary recommendations, advice that is more likely to be followed because of its relevance to Punjabi ways. Henley (1979: 121–45) is one writer who provides health workers with insights into South Asian dietary norms and, to some extent, how these may be linked to the Western nutritional belief system.

Rather than offering advice that violates Punjabi-specific ways, health visitors should aim at offering advice that links Punjabi traditions with Western medical tradition. For example, should a mother consider her body to be more culturally polluted below than above the waist, then advice that includes showering rather than tub-bathing might be more appropriate, thereby allowing for both Punjabi and Western obstetrical codes of hygiene to be upheld simultaneously. The use of flowing water, whether from a jug (*lota*) or a bidet for perineal purposes or from a shower system for bathing purposes, is also part of the Punjabi code of hygiene. The water, as it flows, should move from the purer part of the body to areas that are considered less pure, and not vice versa. As well as the body being divided horizontally (e.g. upper, lower) as to levels of cultural pollution, so the body is divided to some extent vertically, the left hand being considered unclean, and the right hand clean. Food should be eaten and gifts given with the right hand. In the Subcontinent, a physician was noted by the author to dispense medications with the right hand only, following the same rationale. Knowledge relating to which hand is used for various activities has relevance for health visiting, for instance when health visitors demonstrate nappy (diaper) changing or discuss aspects of child development such as fine motor development and handedness. Where Punjabi ways do not align easily with Western scientific ideas on health and illness, the health visitor should support the mother along culture-specific lines, unless for some reason support for a particular practice contravenes the health visitor's code of professional conduct, a situation that health visitors (and all nurses and midwives) face when caring for clients from any cultural tradition.

Among the seventy-two infants born live to the twenty-nine mothers, thirty-nine infants were remembered as being breast-fed, although only twelve for a duration exceeding eight weeks. While four infants (two boys and two girls) born to one mother and raised through infancy in the Subcontinent were breast-fed, each for approximately one year, only six male infants and two female infants raised in the United Kingdom were remembered as being breast-fed for more than two months. The two female infants, who might be considered to be very precious because they were born after several neonatal deaths, were each breast-fed for well over a year. Bearing in mind that, irrespective of religious bias, males are favoured as inheritors in Punjabi society, this finding regarding babies breast-fed for an extended duration suggests that breast-feeding is held in esteem (cf. Dosanjh, 1976: 181; Dobson, 1986: 383). This probable cultural regard for breast-feeding is one factor that a health visitor wishing to encourage a Punjabi mother to breast-feed might emphasize. Another factor is the relaxation that the *chalia* (*sawa maheena*) traditionally provides, the *chalia* being a time when a mother in a joint family household is 'at home all this while' (Dobson, 1987: 337) and can adjust to breast-feeding in the knowledge that her household duties are being cared for by other family members.

In areas where few Punjabi mothers attend antenatal classes, the health visitor might take the opportunity to discover why this is, so that arrangements for relevant antenatal education could be provided in the future. Do Punjabi mothers feel uncomfortable with the type of information discussed in what is in effect a public setting? Do antenatal classes in some localities lack sensitivity to Punjabi cultural norms? With a sense of 'joint family-hood' being usual in addition to parenthood as regards the birth of a Punjabi baby, antenatal education might be considered within collectivist dimensions. It might be that the mother-in-law, who often acts as a mentor in mothercraft during the postpartum period, or a sister-in-law, should be included routinely in invitations to antenatal classes and be encouraged to suggest ideas and vocalize concerns, assured that their views will be warmly received.

Perhaps some families would prefer to watch a videotape on topics relating to pregnancy, childbirth and infant care in the privacy of their home? As many families in the study had video cassette machines and enjoyed watching Indian and Pakistani films, this could be considered a viable possibility. Cassettes could be in both Punjabi and English. A tape which included topics usually covered in antenatal classes, together with ideas relating to the maintenance of Punjabi traditions in hospital and clinic settings, could be made available to families, allowing other family members, the husband and the mother-in-law included, to view the tape in the privacy of their home. For the husband, such a tape would allow him to become informed about current ideas regarding pregnancy, childbirth and infant care without loss of *izzat* by being publicly involved (e.g. by attending antenatal clinics) in what is traditionally exclusively a woman's domain in Punjabi society.

Many of the findings presented in this chapter, whether relating to the Punjabi woman as wife or as mother, may be linked to cultural values relating to authority (senior–junior), gender (male–female), cultural purity (pure–impure) and a concern for cultural danger and vulnerability (Dobson, 1986). In differing situations, some values and not others assume particular importance. For example, when pregnant or recently delivered, the *Bhatra* mother is careful to ensure that her child – whether newborn or in the womb – is safe in cultural terms from harmful forces. Not only does she keep away from anyone who has recently miscarried while she is pregnant lest the pregnancy be affected adversely, but she may keep a much stricter *chalia* for the newborn baby than for herself. Involving as it does childbirth and death, miscarriage is considered to be especially polluting in Punjabi/Indian society (Dobson, 1987: 333; cf. Lozoff, Kamath and Feldman, 1975: 356).

As enduring beliefs, values may sometimes be upheld with tenacity, such as the value that Punjabis accord to female modesty, women, for example, being expected to wear clothing that discreetly covers the female form. Pervading many aspects of a Punjabi woman's life, this value has relevance, as do other Punjabi values, beyond health visiting to nursing practice in general. For instance, not only does the importance placed on female modesty have relevance to the nursing of Punjabi women in intensive care units where patients of both sexes are nursed in one large open area (Parfitt, 1988: 127), but also to uniform worn by Punjabi nurses needing to include trousers (see Mares, Henley and Baxter, 1985: 161–2).

Providing direction to people's lives, cultural values shape numerous decisions people make concerning health and illness. Hence, nurses need insight into their client's cultural value systems, discovering as best they can which values clients consider important in different situations. Rather than reflecting the values of any one member of a cultural group, a cultural value system 'represents what is expected or hoped for, required or forbidden' within a given culture; it is the 'system of criteria by which conduct is judged and sanctions applied' (Albert, 1968: 288). As a means of gaining insight into the client's cultural value system (though not used in the above-described study of Punjabi families), nurses are encouraged by nurse-researchers/educators such as Swanson and Hurley (1983), Brink (1984) and Kanitsaki (1988; see also Burke and Maloney, 1986) to use Kluckhohn's (e.g. Kluckhohn and Strodtbeck, 1961) concept of value orientations in clinical practice. This is described by Swanson and Hurley (1983: 25) as 'a set of dimensions for conceptualizing human beings, their relationship to one another, and place in the universe', one that helps 'differentiate the basic questions all people answer one way or another, largely according to their cultural background'.

Kluckhohn originally isolated five common human problems (derived from the study of philosophy and the philosophy of science) to which 'all peoples at all times and in all

places must find some solution' (Kluckhohn, 1971: 346).
Based on the premise that for each culture there is a
preferential ordering of the three types of solutions that
Kluckhohn (e.g. 1971) suggests exist for each problem, each
culture is considered to have its own distinctive value
orientation profile which most, but not all, its members will
uphold. Due to lack of construct validity (Brink, 1984), the
human nature orientation is no longer included, the four
remaining value orientations and their possible types of
solutions being:

1. *Man–nature orientation*: The problem posed here is what
   is the relation of man to nature (and to supernature)? Also
   described as 'individual–nature' (Tripp-Reimer, 1984: 232)
   and 'person–nature' (Burke and Maloney, 1986: 33), the
   three types of solutions to this problem are: mastery over
   nature, subjugation to nature, and harmony with nature.
2. *Time orientation*: To the problem 'What is the temporal
   focus of human life?', the three types of solutions are:
   future, present and past.
3. *Activity orientation*: This problem is concerned with the
   mode of human activity. The three types of solutions
   towards which human activity may be oriented are:
   being, being-in-becoming and doing.
4. *Relational orientation*: This problem is concerned with a
   person's relationship to other people, the three types of
   solutions being: collateral, lineal and individualistic (see
   Tripp-Reimer, 1984; Burke and Maloney, 1986).

Drawing on her research and relating each of the four
value orientations in turn to the cultural world of the Anang
people of Nigeria, Brink (1984) envisages nurses using
Kluckhohn's (1971: 345) idea of a 'value orientation profile'
to help establish the cultural values and beliefs of both
client and nurse with the intent to discover whether they
may anticipate an agreement or a conflict of values (Brink,
1984: 198, 200). While cultural differences in value orientations held by nurse and client may present more forcefully
than do cultural similarities, both are nevertheless important. The recognition of commonalities in one or more
orientations can provide a useful basis for mutual under-

standing in intercultural situations as nurse and client seek to understand and bridge cultural differences.

As well as gaining insight into the client's culture by using assessment tools designed specifically to elicit cultural information such as Kluckhohn's (Kluckhohn and Strodtbeck, 1961) tool for assessing value orientations, nurses can gain useful insights by giving emphasis to cultural factors when using other client assessment tools. Genograms and ecomaps are two such tools, tools that allow for a wide range of client information relating to health and social support systems to be combined and presented in an easy to comprehend, graphic manner. The genogram provides an historical perspective of the client's life situation, while the ecomap offers an ecological perspective, that is, a view of a family's or an individual's interactions with their external environment (see, e.g. Hartman, 1978; Wright and Leahey, 1984: 30–8; Dobson, 1989b). When using either tool, emphasis can be given to cultural information.

Resembling a family tree and usually extending over three generations, the genogram provides the nurse with a format for gathering together a variety of information about the client's extended family, information such as age, kinship relationships, occupations, ethnic group, religious affiliation, marital status and pertinent health information (e.g. who has or is known to have had cardiovascular conditions, cancer, or diabetes mellitus; who are/were smokers). When using the genogram in intercultural situations, nurses need to be alert to differences in terms used in different cultures to describe members of the extended family. Cultural variations also exist regarding which relatives traditionally reside together, some perhaps sharing the same hearth or stove as well as the same living area or compound (see e.g. Barnard and Good, 1984: 78–81). At times, a nurse may find it helpful to encircle those relatives who under ideal, traditional circumstances would reside together, and also the situation as it is in reality. Where it becomes apparent that a client lacks the geographical proximity of family members with whom it is customary to reside in close proximity, and thus be at hand to offer support in times of need such as during sickness and old age, the nurse is better able to

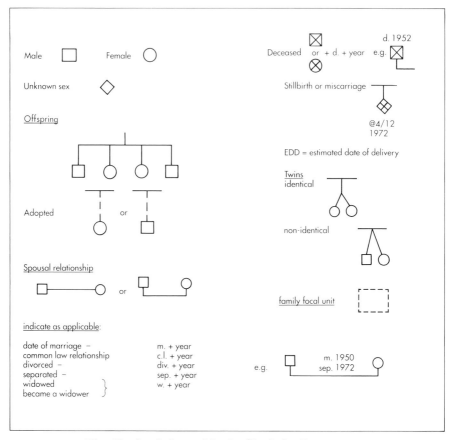

Fig. 20   Symbols used in the Singh family genogram

foresee potential difficulties that might arise and so help a client form contingency plans.

A nurse interested in cultural factors relating to specific times in a client's lifespan, such as pregnancy and childbirth, might find it helpful to use a system of colour coding to highlight specific information. In regard to pregnancy and childbirth, for example, the nurse caring for a woman pregnant for the first time might highlight those family members who, by tradition, would guide and support the client through pregnancy, childbirth and the early years of

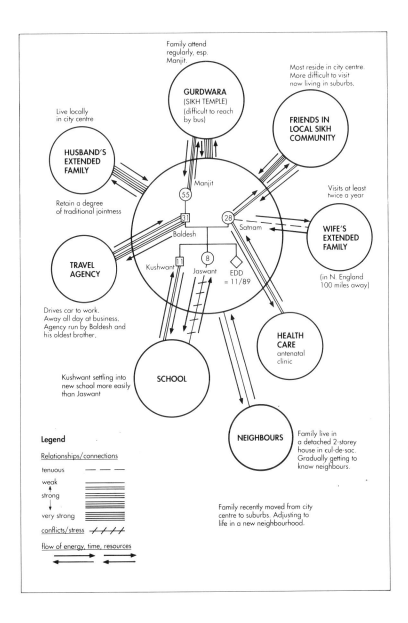

Fig. 21 The Singh family – Ecomap

childrearing as well as those who in reality will act as mentors. It may also be relevant to highlight family members who have delivered with the assistance of traditional midwives as well as children and siblings who have been breast-fed. In another genogram, the focus might be on the family's use of, and involvement in, traditional health practices, perhaps indicating which members are, or have been, important within the extended family for providing advice regarding treatments and remedies for various illnesses and conditions and/or for helping others cope with emotional, social and spiritual problems. In addition, the nurse might note which family members use, or are remembered as using, alternative therapies and/or healers, that is healers who follow an approach to care and cure that differs from the country's dominant approach. In countries where Western scientific medicine dominates, alternative therapies might include *tai chi*, yoga and acupuncture, while alternative healers might include chiropractors, faith healers and *hakims*.

Rather than providing a graphic overview, as does the genogram, of a family's or an individual client's health and social situation in historical terms, the ecomap provides an overview in ecological terms. Drawing on systems theory, the ecomap is a visual summary of a family's or an individual's relationship with their external environment. Not only does it point up family strengths, but identifies stressful situations and conflicts that exist between the client's system (whether relating to the family-as-client or to an individual client) and systems within the client's external environment. Schematically, the ecomap consists of a large, centrally placed circle which represents the client system, around which smaller circles are drawn, each smaller circle representing an important part of the client's external environment. These other systems, which vary from family to family (or, where applicable, from individual to individual), may include neighbours, a church group, a child's school, friends, a wife's and/or husband's natal family, a mother's and/or a father's workplace, and even the family pet. Relationships and connections between these systems – whether strong, weak or tenuous, whether consuming much

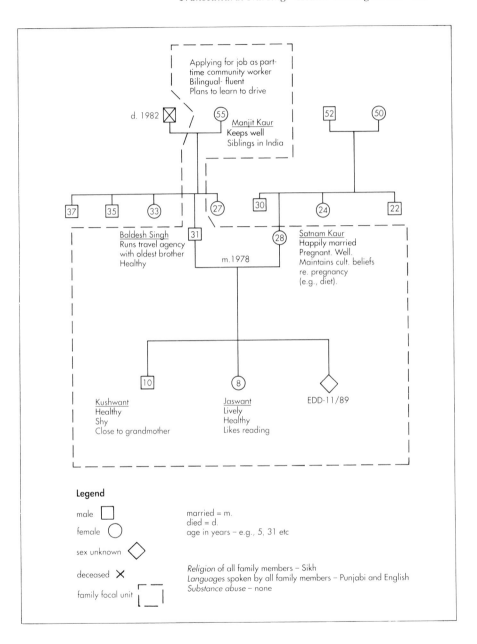

Fig. 22 The Singh family – Genogram

or little time and energy, and whether riven by conflict – are symbolized by the use of bands of lines, arrows and slash marks.

For many ethnic minority families, their ecomap will identify connections they maintain not only with systems within their ethnic minority community, such as ethnic minority clubs and churches, but also with systems within the wider environment, such as major health care and educational services that serve the population at large. Whether used on only one occasion or in serial fashion, ecomaps provide a very visual way in which to help an individual or a family look at his/her/its social world and consider how this is changing, and hence can be used to assist a new immigrant or immigrant family think through ways of settling into a new and different cultural milieu, while retaining their own sense of ethnic identity.

TRANSCULTURAL NURSING: A CONTEMPORARY IMPERATIVE

While many health visitors may be unfamiliar with cultural traditions upheld by Punjabi families, such traditions, and those of Britain's other ethnic minority groups, are all part of the fabric of contemporary British society. Health visitors familiar with their client's culture, and in relation to the above discussion with Punjabi culture, will be much more able to provide care that has relevance to the client's culture and to develop health visitor–client relationships built on understanding and respect for each other's culture. Throughout the world, nurses care for multicultural populations and need to work skilfully across cultural differences if they are to provide a caring, client-centred service. But to deliver culturally sensitive care to clients of all ages and with various health needs and concerns, nurses require educational preparation for that purpose and an organizational milieu in which transcultural nursing is actively promoted and supported. Nurses should not be as 'lone eagles', striving to deliver transcultural nursing care without active support from their employers, nor should they

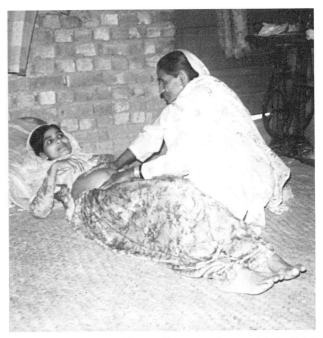

Fig. 23   A midwife attending a client on a home visit in Pakistan

lack the opportunity to develop expertise in transcultural
nursing within a nurse educational setting, whether as basic
or continuing nurse education.

Transcultural nursing involves understanding and helping 'cultural groups with their nursing and health care
needs with full thought to culture-specific values, beliefs and
practices' (Leininger, 1978: 8). Codes of professional conduct
and ethics for nursing, such as those published in the United
Kingdom (UKCC, 1984) and Canada (CNA, 1989), include
clauses which highlight cultural factors among those which
nurses must consider when providing client care. In this
text, transcultural nursing involves special emphasis being
given to the idea of nurses *respecting* their client's culture
and providing culturally sensitive and relevant care in a
caring manner. Furthermore, transcultural nursing is envisaged as an approach to client care in which *all* nurses,
rather than a selected few, develop proficiency and become

increasingly able to offer culturally sensitive care to clients from diverse cultures. This is not to state that nurses are envisaged as working easily and effectively with all clients from cultures other than their own all of the time, but that they have an understanding of the concept of culture in relation to ethnic grouping and its pervasiveness in all aspects of living, including health and illness, and have been prepared educationally to provide culturally sensitive care in inter- as well as intracultural situations. Nurses with special expertise in caring for members of a particular ethnic group are valued as sources of reference for other nurses, being able to offer nursing advice on culturally complex situations relating to members of the ethnic group in question.

Hallmarked by the reciprocation of cultural knowledge and respect (or 'transcultural reciprocity') (Dobson, 1989c), transcultural nursing involves an affirmative desire by the nurse both to bridge and transcend cultural differences where a cultural disparity exists in the nurse–client relationship. Far from being an approach used only by nurses from the ethnic majority when caring for ethnic minority clients, transcultural nursing is seen as an approach for *all* nurses to use when caring for clients from cultures other than their own. However, if transcultural nursing is to be the participative, intercultural process that it is intended to be, then it involves nurses winning their client's trust in them as confidential, caring and culturally concerned practitioners. This then is part of the challenge of transcultural nursing, for should the client be reluctant to share information relating to his/her cultural ways, the nurse will have difficulty in reaching a diagnosis based on culturally accurate information and in planning and providing culturally aligned care.

Although nursing is frequently described as a reciprocal process, the concept of reciprocity has not received the in-depth consideration that its central position in nursing practice warrants (see e.g. Chapman (1980) regarding the concept of 'social exchange' in relation to nursing, and Dobson (1989c) regarding 'transcultural reciprocity'). Viewed within cultural parameters, several of Travelbee's

(1971) ideas may be considered useful in providing insight into the concept of reciprocity in transcultural nursing, for example Travelbee's (ibid.: 132) notion of 'emerging identities'. This idea involves the nurse being 'able to transcend herself to some extent' in order to perceive the 'uniqueness' of the other person and 'to establish a bond' with that person (ibid.: 132, 135). Travelbee (p. 203) also develops the idea of a person being able to expand his/her 'empathic boundaries' in order to develop empathy with those who are dissimilar to him/herself. It is suggested (Dobson, 1989c: 101) that a number of sub-concepts: for example, 'respect' and 'empathy', subsume the concept of transcultural reciprocity and require serious consideration as they relate to transcultural nursing practice.

In today's world where nurses frequently find themselves in intercultural nurse–client situations, it is vital that nurses have insight into cultures other than their own if their client assessments are to be culturally astute. While the literature provides much useful information relevant to a wide range of cultural groups, cultures are dynamic entities and individual clients vary as to the extent to which they adhere to traditions and values of their cultural heritage. Therefore, to practise effectively within transcultural dimensions, nurses must be adept in their everyday practice at collecting and collating pertinent information relating to their client's culture, and, thereafter, be skilled in blending this information imaginatively and caringly into the care they offer. As nurse and client in a multicultural society may each belong to one of a variety of cultural traditions, nurse–client relationships may involve a wide range of cultural disparities. With the ethnic identity of both client and nurse determining whether or not transcultural nursing skills and abilities are needed in client care, ethnic identity is an important form of client identification in multicultural societies, self-definition by the client being one approach that nurses might use to determine the client's ethnic identity. The nurse must also be aware of his/her own ethnic identity and consider how this influences his/her nursing practice.

Transcultural nursing addresses but one of a range of

possible disparities between client and nurse. Various differences, such as race, class and gender as well as culture, may exist, one or more of which may impede, each in its own way, nurse–client understanding and the provision of client-oriented nursing care. Transcending such differences is an important challenge that nurses share with other health professionals, and one that needs to be discussed openly when nurses work in interdisciplinary teams. Clients from racial minorities who have faced racial prejudice and who fear the possibility of racial discrimination may understandably be reluctant to share their ideas and cultural knowledge with a nurse from the majority culture, which in many Western countries is predominantly white. Although transcultural nursing is not seen to encompass 'transracial nursing' (a term that is rarely used, preference usually being given to 'multiracial' (e.g. Mares, Henley and Baxter, 1985) or nursing 'ethnic people of color' (Branch and Paxton, 1976)), the need for both transcultural and transracial sensitivity may be required simultaneously: the idea of caring for another person irrespective of differences, be they cultural and/or racial, is fundamental to both intercultural and interracial nursing situations. It is also important that emphasis on cultural factors does not lead to ethnic minority cultures being seen as inadequate and their practices as inferior, nor that realities of racial discrimination (covert as well as overt) which preclude members of racial minority groups from access to quality health care are glossed over (see in regard to the United Kingdom: Satow and Homans, 1982; Mares, Henley and Baxter, 1985; Pearson, 1986).

The sense of powerlessness that many racial/cultural minority groups feel when faced with the dominating power of major bureaucratic social institutions, such as the British health care services, is a reality that nurses must be cognisant of and sensitive to when practising within the transcultural mode (see Bruni, 1988, regarding Australia; O'Neil, 1986, regarding Canada). Such organizations are often unicultural in nature; that is, the primacy of the dominant culture is upheld with only peripheral recognition given to other cultural groups in society. It is not surprising in view of this felt, and often real, lack of empowerment that many racial/cultural minority groups wish to be active in shaping and developing health care services that meet their needs, culturally and racially. One group who provided medical and nursing care for its own members in days past were the Doukhobors, a religio-cultural group who arrived from Russia and settled on the Canadian prairies during the 1800s (Gibbon, 1947: 209). More recently, Joan Winch, an Australian Aborigine nurse, has been active in developing community health services geared specifically to the needs and culture of Australian Aborigines in Western Australia (Crabbe, 1989; also Winch, 1989). Being able to identify closely with those who provide their nursing care is immensely important to many members of cultural/racial minority groups, as it is for those of the majority culture, providing the individual and/or the group as a whole with a sense of certainty that one's life experiences will be understood and one's cultural ways will not be viewed askance.

All nurses in multicultural societies, whether they are in nursing practice, education, administration or research, have a part to play in ensuring that nursing can be, and is, practised with cultural sensitivity and that transcultural expertise becomes part of each nurse's repertoire of approaches to client care. Nurse researchers and scholars, for instance, are needed to clarify and explore issues and concerns that relate to differing aspects of transcultural nursing, such as the ability of nursing faculty to teach about cultural differences (Jaffe Ruiz, 1981). Many questions need to be asked, including whether clients' cultural ways are being considered routinely in the provision of nursing care. To what extent are clients from ethnic minority groups expected to acquiesce in the ways of the majority culture with little or no consideration being given to their own cultural ways? Does the nursing profession take for granted that ideas and innovations for nursing practice which have been generated within the ethos of the majority culture will automatically be acceptable to a multicultural populace? Do members of ethnic minority communities have avenues for effectively channelling their needs and concerns to the nursing profession, and, if so, what priority is accorded to those concerns? Questions such as these need to be raised and concerns of ethnic minority groups openly addressed not only by the practising nurse, but also by nurse leaders whose policies help to shape the practice of nursing and who are influential in deciding what resources will be allocated, when and to whom. 'Bringing culture into care' (Dobson, 1983) involves nurses in all areas and at all levels of nursing in recognizing that health is culturally defined, that each one of us is a cultural being, and that nursing care should be culturally relevant to the needs and circumstance of the client, whether an individual, a family, or a community.

Over the past several decades, transcultural nursing has emerged as a dynamic and caring approach to nursing that acknowledges the importance of cultural factors to sensitive and efficacious client care. In a world where more people than ever before travel abroad, whether for economic, educational or political reasons or to enjoy a vacation in fresh surroundings, and with many countries being multi-cultural in composition, the nurse of today needs to be a transculturally proficient practitioner if s/he is to provide a truly caring service for a culturally diverse clientele. As an approach to practice that requires the practitioner to provide nursing care which has meaning for the client in the context of the client's culture, transcultural nursing has become nothing less than a contemporary imperative. The practitioner is not alone in being responsible for the provision of culturally sensitive nursing care, for the input, support and direction of nurse administrators, educators and researchers are vital too.

REFERENCES

Community Health Nursing – Health Visiting

CETHV (Council for the Education and Training of Health Visitors) (1977) *An Investigation into the Principles of Health Visiting*. London: CETHV.

Gibbon JM (1947) *Three Centuries of Canadian Nursing*. Toronto: Macmillan.

McCleary GF (1935) *The Maternity and Child Welfare Movement*. London: P.S. King & Son.

McClymont M, Thomas S and Denham MJ (1986) *Health Visiting and the Elderly*. Edinburgh: Churchill Livingstone.

Orr J (1985) Assessing individual and family health needs. In K Luker and J Orr (eds), *Health Visiting*, Oxford: Blackwell Scientific Publications.

Rattray J (1961) *Great Days in New Zealand Nursing*. London: Harrap.

RCN (Royal College of Nursing) (1971) *Report of the Working Party on the Role of the Health Visitor Now and in a Changing National Health Service*. London: RCN.

UKCC (United Kingdom Central Council for Nursing, Midwifery and Health Visiting) (1984) *Code of Professional Conduct for the Nurse, Midwife and Health Visitor*, 2nd edn. London: UKCC.

United Kingdom. Laws, Statutes, etc. (1946) *National Health Service Act*. 9 and 10 George 6, ch. 81. London: HMSO.

Maternal and Child Health Visiting – Caring for Punjabi Families

Albert EM (1968) Values – II. Value systems. In DL Sills (ed.), *International Encyclopaedia of the Social Sciences*, **16**. New York: Macmillan/Free Press.

Anonymous (1980) Personal communication. Health professional.

Anonymous (1986) Personal communication. Adult female Punjabi living in the United Kingdom.

Anwar M (1979) *The Myth of Return. Pakistanis in Britain*. London: Heinemann.

Atkinson J (1971) *A Handbook for Interviewers*. London: HMSO.

Barnard A and Good A (1984) *Research Practices in the Study of Kinship*. London: Academic Press.

Bell RT (1968) The Indian background. In R Oakley (ed.), *New Backgrounds. The immigrant child at home and at school*, London: Oxford University Press.

Bott E (1957) *Family and Social Network*. London: Tavistock.

Brink PJ (1984) Value orientations as an assessment tool in cultural diversity. *Nursing Research* **33**(4): 198–203.

Burke SO and Maloney R (1986) The women's value orientation questionnaire. An instrument revision study. *Nursing Papers* **18**(1): 32–44.

Carnevali DL (1983) *Nursing Care Planning. Diagnosis and management*, 3rd edn. Philadelphia: Lippincott.

Clark J (1985) *The Process of Health Visiting*. Unpublished PhD thesis, Council for National Academic Awards, Polytechnic of the South Bank, London.

Dobson S (1985) Under a Punjabi sky. *Nursing Times* **81**(7): 44–6.

Dobson S (1986) Cultural value awareness. Glimpses into a Punjabi mother's world. *Health Visitor* **59**(12): 382–4.

Dobson SM (1987) *The Role of the Health Visitor in Multi-cultural Situations.* Unpublished PhD thesis, University of Edinburgh.

Dobson SM (1988a) Transcultural health visiting. Caring in a multi-cultural society. *Recent Advances in Nursing* **20**, 61–80.

Dobson SM (1988b) Ethnic identity. A basis for care. *Midwife, Health Visitor and Community Nurse* **24**(5): 172, 176, 178.

Dobson SM (1989a) Visiting the Punjabi mother as wife and community member. *Focus* [Scottish HVA magazine], No. 14, 6–9.

Dobson SM (1989b) Genograms and ecomaps. *Nursing Times* **85**(51): 54–6.

Dosanjh JS (1976) *A Comparative Study of Punjabi and English Child Rearing Practices with Special Reference to Lower Juniors (7–9 years).* Unpublished PhD thesis, University of Nottingham.

Gideon H (1962) A baby is born in the Punjab. *American Anthropologist* **64**(6):1220–34.

Hartman A (1978) Diagrammatic assessment of family relationships. *Social Casework* **59**(8): 465–76.

Henley A (1979) *Asian Patients in Hospital and at Home.* London: King Edward's Hospital Fund for London.

Henley A (1982) *Asians in Britain. Caring for Muslims and their families: religious aspects of care.* London: DHSS/King Edward's Hospital Fund for London.

Henley A (1983) *Asians in Britain. Caring for Sikhs and their families: religious aspects of care.* London: DHSS/King Edward's Hospital Fund for London.

Homans H (1982) Pregnancy and birth as rites of passage for two groups of women in Britain. In CP MacCormack (ed.), *Ethnography of Fertility and Birth*, London: Academic Press.

Homans H (1983) A question of balance. Asian and British women's perceptions of food during pregnancy. In A Murcott (ed.), *The Sociology of Food and Eating. Essays on the social significance of food*, Aldershot: Gower.

Iqbal M (ed.) (1981) *East Meets West. A background to some Asian faiths.* London: Commission for Racial Equality.

Jones AD and Dougherty C (1982) Childbirth in a scientific and industrial society. In CP MacCormack (ed.), *Ethnography of Fertility and Birth*, London: Academic Press.

Kanitsaki O (1988) Transcultural nursing. Challenge to change. *The Australian Journal of Advanced Nursing* **5**(3): 4–11.

Kluckhohn FR (1971) Dominant and variant value orientations. In

C Kluckhohn and HA Murray (eds), *Personality in Nature, Society, and Culture*, 2nd edn, New York: Knopf.

Kluckhohn FR and Strodtbeck FL (1961) *Variations in Value Orientations*. Evanston, IL: Row, Peterson.

Lozoff B, Kamath KR and Feldman RA (1975) Infection and disease in South Indian families. Beliefs about childhood diarrhea. *Human Organization* **34**(4): 353–8.

Mares P, Henley A and Baxter C (1985) *Health Care in Multiracial Britain*. Cambridge: Health Education Council/National Extension College.

Moser CA and Kalton G (1971) *Survey Methods in Social Investigation*, 2nd edn. London: Heinemann.

Nichter M and Nichter M (1983) The ethnophysiology and folk dietetics of pregnancy. A case study from South India. *Human Organization* **42**(3): 235–46.

Orr J (1980) *Health Visiting in Focus. A consumer view of health visiting in Northern Ireland*. London: Royal College of Nursing.

Parfitt BA (1988) Cultural assessment in the intensive care unit. *Intensive Care Nursing* **4**(3): 124–7.

Sampson C (1982) *The Neglected Ethic. Religious and cultural factors in the care of patients*. London: McGraw-Hill.

Singh H (1977) *Bhatra Sikhs in Bristol. Development of an ethnic community*. Unpublished dissertation as part of BSc degree, Dept of Sociology, University of Bristol.

Staton M (1981) Churching. Past and present. *Contact* [Journal of Pastoral Studies]. No. 72, 10–17.

Swanson AR and Hurley PM (1983) Family systems. Values and value conflicts. *Journal of Psychosocial Nursing and Mental Health Services* **21**(7): 24–30.

Tripp-Reimer T (1984) Cultural assessment. In JP Bellack and PA Bamford (eds), *Nursing Assessment. A multidimensional approach*, Monterey, CA: Wadsworth.

Wakil PA (1970) Explorations into the kin-networks of the Punjabi society. A preliminary statement. *Journal of Marriage and the Family* **32**(4): 700–7.

Werbner P (1979) *Ritual and Social Networks. A study of Pakistani immigrants in Manchester*. Unpublished PhD thesis, University of Manchester.

Wright LM and Leahey M (1984) *Nurses and Families. A guide to family assessment and intervention*. Philadelphia: Davis.

Transcultural Nursing – Contemporary Imperative

Branch MF and Paxton PP (eds) (1976) *Providing Safe Nursing*

Care for Ethnic People of Color. New York: Appleton-Century-Crofts.

Bruni N (1988) A critical analysis of transcultural theory. *The Australian Journal of Advanced Nursing* 5(3): 26–32.

Chapman CM (1980) The rights and responsibilities of nurses and patients. *Journal of Advanced Nursing* 5(2): 127–34.

CNA (Canadian Nurses Association) (1989) *Code of Ethics for Nursing.* Ottawa: CNA.

Crabbe G (1989) Healing the dreamers. *Nursing Times* 85(13): 16–17.

Dobson S (1983) Bringing culture into care. *Nursing Times* 79(6): 53, 56–7.

Dobson SM (1989c) Conceptualizing for transcultural health visiting. The concept of transcultural reciprocity. *Journal of Advanced Nursing* 14: 97–102.

Gibbon JM (1947) *Three Centuries of Canadian Nursing.* Toronto: Macmillan.

Jaffe Ruiz MC (1981) Open-closed mindedness, intolerance of ambiguity and nursing faculty attitudes toward culturally different patients. *Nursing Research* 30(3): 177–81.

Leininger M (1978) Transcultural nursing. A new and scientific subfield of study in nursing. In M Leininger (ed.), *Transcultural Nursing. Concepts, theories, and practices*, New York: John Wiley.

Mares P, Henley A and Baxter C (1985) *Health Care in Multiracial Britain.* Cambridge: Health Education Council/National Extension College.

O'Neil JD (1986) The politics of health in the Fourth World. A northern Canadian example. *Human Organization* 45(2): 119–28.

Pearson M (1986) The politics of ethnic minority health studies. In T Rathwell and D Phillips (eds), *Health, Race and Ethnicity*, London: Croom Helm.

Satow A and Homans H (1982) Fair service for all. *Journal of Community Nursing*, February 5(8): 19–22.

Travelbee J (1971) *Interpersonal Aspects of Nursing*, 2nd edn. Philadelphia: FA Davis.

UKCC (United Kingdom Central Council for Nursing, Midwifery and Health Visiting) (1984) *Code of Professional Conduct for the Nurse, Midwife and Health Visitor*, 2nd edn. London: UKCC.

Winch J (1989) Why is health care for Aborigines so ineffective? In *Issues in Australian Nursing – 2.* G Gray and R Pratt (eds), Melbourne: Churchill Livingstone.

Index

abdominal stoma, effect of on
 Muslim, 38
activity orientation
 (Kluckhohn), 170
Acts of Parliament
 Canada, Canadian
  Multiculturalism Act (1988), 9
 United Kingdom, Aliens Act
  (1905), 5–6, National Health
  Service Act (1946), 147
 United States of America,
  Exclusion Act (1882), 16
acupuncture, 174
adaptive model of health, 41
Africans, abduction of into slave
 trade, 18
Afro-Caribbean people, 55
Aliens Act 1905 (UK), 5–6
Aleut, 19
alternative therapies, 174
American Indians
 definition of, 16–17
 Muckleshoot, 20
 Navaho/Navajo, 20, 116
Amish, 102
Anang of Nigeria, 170
antenatal classes/education, 167–8
 uptake of by Punjabi mothers,
  156, 159
antenatal traditions, 154–6
antenatal visiting, 148, 159
anthropology, 86–90
 medical anthropology, 87–8

and nurse education, 83, 87
and nursing, 66, 85–90
anti-rickets campaign, in Asian
 community (UK), 81
Appalachian, 66
Arabs, in USA, 20
Arain sub-caste, 151, 153
articles of faith, 5 Ks of Sikhism,
 150–1
Asian Indians
 and anti-rickets campaign, 81
 attitude to diarrhoea/
  dehydration, 51–2
 in Canada, 10, 12
 in United Kingdom, 53, 55, 79–81,
  see also Punjabis
 in United States of America, 19
Association of Nurses and
 Anthropologists (UK), 85
attitude
 of nurse to culturally different
  patient, 68
 racist, 6
Australia, 24–6
Australian aborigines, 24–6,
 116, 181
azan (Muslim call to prayer), 157

baba, 155
Baha'i faith, 15
Bangladeshi, 7, 80
 Muslim, 114
Basque people, 21